COMING FOR
MONEY

COMING FOR
MONEY

A NOVEL OF INTERNATIONAL FINANCE

F.W. vom Scheidt

Blue Butterfly Books

THINK FREE, BE FREE

Blue Butterfly Book Publishing Inc.
2583 Lakeshore Boulevard West, Toronto, Ontario, Canada M8V 1G3
Tel 416-255-3930   Fax 416-252-8291   www.bluebutterflybooks.ca

Complete ordering information for Blue Butterfly titles is available at:
www.bluebutterflybooks.ca

First edition, soft cover: 2009

LIBRARY AND ARCHIVES CANADA CATALOGUING IN PUBLICATION

Vom Scheidt, F. W. (Frederick William), 1951–
Coming for money : a novel of international finance / F. W. vom Scheidt.

ISBN 978-0-9784982-8-3

I. Title.

PS8643.O48C56 2009   C813'.6   C2009-900120-9

Design and typesetting by Gary Long / Fox Meadow Creations
Text set in Warnock

Printed and bound in Canada by Transcontinental-Métrolitho

The text paper in this book, Rolland Enviro 100 from Cascades, is EcoLogo™ and Forest Stewardship Council certified. It contains 100 per cent post-consumer recycled fibre, was processed chlorine free, and was manufactured using energy from biogas recovered from a municipal landfill site.

No government grants were sought or received in connection with the publication of this book. Blue Butterfly Books thanks its patrons for their support in the marketplace.

For Eileen

CAPHIS: *Good even, Varro. What! You come for money?*
VARRO SERVANT: *Is't not your business too?*
CAPHIS: *It is...*

  —WILLIAM SHAKESPEARE
  Timon of Athens, ACT III, SCENE IV

I do not know how to distinguish between our waking life and a dream. Are we not always living the life that we imagine we are?

—HENRY DAVID THOREAU

1

Some days it felt like the money left blood on my hands.

Not the weary allusion to the stains of Iscariot.

Sometimes, when my complex calculations penetrated its sly whispers of profit, like the smears on the latex gloves of a surgeon probing a body laid open and breathing beneath sure fingers.

Sometimes, when I pounded its promises into the phone, like the flecks blown back into the clenched knuckles of an assassin working too close to the throat.

Most often like seared blisters blossoming from the soft centre of your palms when working wood or rope without the protection of leather, because the devastating urgency of profit or loss arrived as a crisis in a storm and you had no other choice but to grapple with it to the exclusion of everything else; lose your grip, lose your life.

That was always how I visualized it, the money—as a storm raging: billowing from one trading market in the world to another as the sun passed from Tokyo to Hong Kong, relentless in its advance to Frankfurt, across the Channel to London, and then on to New York and Toronto, and continually westward to Asia again. Sudden squalls at opening bells that drove us, investment bankers, like ardent navigators at lurching helms, whipping the financial markets up into floods of trading, and then passing, on the closing bell, without pause or caring or conscience.

Always, the pace of it made me feel I was vanishing into myself.

Why I could never quit—when I was so unremittingly reminded by the velocity of the money that there was no end; that there were no enduring winners or losers; that, finally, no one prevailed; and that, like the process of life itself, nothing was permanent—I was unable to fully understand, despite my rigid pursuit of an answer.

My understanding always remained hemmed in by my recognition that I was better at it, the money, than anything else I did. Skilled. I could manipulate it with my intellect. Shave a single investment transaction into a hundred layers, thin as onion skin, translucent, all the profit and loss exposed. Then remould them into a solution, dead simple, unerringly profitable.

And sometimes I could operate on instinct fleeter than intellect, my feet never having to touch the ground.

But none of it was meaningful enough to explain why I kept hanging on. That was all I was doing any more. My determination to succeed reduced to a determination not to surrender.

I sat in my office.

Alone.

I let my fingertips leave the arms of my chair to touch the rim of my desk with both hands meeting, attempting to complete myself in the circle of their joining. The slight nervous habit had become a trusted routine for holding myself firm in a pulling tide of unease.

I was tired. I needed to sleep; not just wait out the night, a pit of hollow shadows and scraps of dreams when I closed my eyes.

I needed to stop moving. I needed to stop feeling that, like a shark, I had to have continuous restless movement to maintain my breathing.

I caught myself listening to the curtain of stillness in the empty office. Everyone had long departed. In their departure, the daily accumulation of noise and vibration and frenzy had been deflated out of the rooms and cubicles and corridors. The cleaning staff, with their hum of carpet vacuums and soft whoosh of emptied paper shredders, had already trooped through. The lull pushed back against my listening.

It was almost ten, the leavings of the day shrinking towards midnight.

I shoved my heels out beneath my desk, lifting myself on them, and leaned back into my chair. I stretched savagely, striking jagged pain into my knees and shoulders, attempting without success to dispel the doubts seated within me, as unbreakable as stones.

Dropping back down, I looked to the creased calendar page of my desk diary. Days fenced within squares—neither their number nor their duration to be altered despite my wanting. Seven months to this day since it happened, leaving me with lop-sided anniversaries: Friday bending each week; the twenty-first day bringing a false stop to each month. And also leaving me pursued by an internal voice that had begun speaking within me since that day (reduced to "that day" by the voice). An unfamiliar voice, maybe reclaimed from an invented self of distant childhood, it leaked through the cracks and gaps between my thoughts. I could not turn it off the way I turned my thoughts off, or turned them to something else; persistent, sceptical, the voice crowded my thoughts with words I could not speak out loud to anyone.

Tonight, the voice stalked my solitude, interrupting my

thoughts each time they began to settle, causing a flutter of fear within me, like a sharp noise jerking me awake just as I was falling asleep. It fed a stubborn suspicion that it was becoming possible for me to lose my grip on my ambition and accomplishments, and let my interrupted life diminish to nothing.

Sitting there, edgy and worn, I tried to dispel the voice and prove it false, tried to prove my life still had some substance by compiling a mental list of my achievements. I was hard pressed to show anything for the past seven months; baskets without bottoms that the days had fallen through, and were then lost. Lately, I had tried to fabricate some refuge within a detached acceptance: in the end, what did anybody have to show for the time before their lights went out? But that was an open-ended question that brought me no closer to any answers. Nor did it serve me tonight with any fresh truth.

My day was run out. My week was run out. I felt no further from my past, no closer to my future.

Outside the tall narrow windows, with the surrounding office towers gone mostly cold and black, the darkness folded around the glass, squeezing in the light, turning my gaze back at me.

Within, my computer screen cast feathery ripples of brightness that lapped at my wrists. Its metallic incandescence seemed a digital fire, keeping predators at bay. It also brought forth an enticing murmur of distant bonds and treasury bills that trolled through my idleness, luring up the darting fish of my trading reflexes.

I tapped up a cluster of Bloomberg screens that tracked twenty-four-hour global futures and foreign exchange markets, the incoming trades stacking up for execution on a Monday morning that would begin in Asia while we remained stuck behind the starting gate on Sunday night.

The procession of numbers painted a series of portraits. A

Tokyo stock market that would sweat under the exertion of massive trading volumes in its opening hour. Currency markets in Singapore and Hong Kong that would take faltering initial steps in their pursuit of the previous week's money trails. The luminous computer screens giving me windows into a day not yet arrived in the world. One window tumbling onto the next at the command of my impatient fingertips, like cards dealt from a deck.

The screens were alive with stacks of iridescent numerals that popped and jiggled like electric fleas spilled from an open box, and with fluorescent sticks of lightning undulating up and down on charts and graphs; all monitoring and measuring, in ceaseless statistics and averages and returns, the vital pulse of the money. In this through-the-looking-glass image of commerce and trade, there was no evidence of human life—only the outcome of harvests taken from fields or minerals hauled from mine shafts, loaded onto trains and ships, processed in plants and factories; sold; and repeatedly sold again; no sense of intent, no sense of labour, no sense of use—only a precise chronicle of the profit and loss that accrued at each stage.

Flipping through more screens produced a rainstorm of numbers and computations: bonds bought, stocks sold, currencies traded this day, wheat and corn to change hands next month, gold and silver promised for delivery at year end.

In the hyperactivity of the numbers there was a powerful pornography of betting and winning or losing, lurid and selfish and seductive. I drew the flow into myself, inflating my veins and arteries with the short-lived tension of profit and loss, an invalid plasma without sufficient substance to sustain life.

When I became aware of the telephone buzzing on the corner of my desk, I knew I had, within those moments, become so deeply entangled in the screens I had missed the initial trills.

My direct line flashed. I reached quickly, awkwardly off balance from bending so deeply into my computer screen. Racing my gummy tongue across the day's accumulation of coffee on my teeth, I scooped up the handset and closed it to my face.

"This is Paris," I answered.

I listened intently, without interrupting, repeatedly pressing my upper teeth against my lower.

"Okay," I replied. "Do it. Do it now."

Without waiting for any response, I hung up.

And my hands?

I let them hang, jittery at my wrists, static in my fingertips.

I could not go away from who I was.

2

On weekends, I seemed to live a breath at a time.

Saturday and Sunday inched by in a downward spiral, making me increasingly edgy. Fickle. Channel surfing till dawn. Feeling it in some part of every minute, the need to reach the hurry of days with deadlines waiting in the coming week on the other side.

When I could no longer tolerate the inertia that accumulated, like a surely rising tide from the moment of leaving the office Friday night, I grudgingly sought the support of a familiar arm-chair and the distraction of whisky in my hand.

In my memory were weekends that flowed like a glassy river from Friday to Monday; the living room a tranquil anchorage, ripe with the indolence of fat newspapers, rich coffee, and flaky pastry crumbs.

Any more, I found I could only look outwards.

At my elbow, the panelled windows of my twentieth-floor condominium let in the last city views, wavering in the watery light of the late winter afternoon.

I swirled the glass in my hand, bringing forth the familiar and reassuring rattle of the ice cubes.

"It was even easier than I expected," I announced above the knocking ice cubes, one thought present, all others absent. "All

I had to do was be patient. Not run scared. Wait out the week, and give them just enough rope to hang themselves."

I kept my eyes on a distant point where the chilly winter sky blurred with the skyline.

"You know what?" I asked her.

I pulled a trickle of Scotch off the rim of my glass, let it warm behind my teeth before I swallowed it slowly. "I knew they'd oversubscribe those bonds. I knew they'd see the dollar signs stacking up before their eyes like sugarplums. That bank has always been run from head office in Amsterdam by the greediest bunch of bastards I've ever seen. They'd sell twice as many bonds as they could get their hands on. Three times as many. They wouldn't care. They'd do it just to keep the bidding juicy."

Eagerly, I began to re-climb the steps of my success, the sensations free-flowing within me, the adrenaline of the risk, the elation of winning.

I sipped again. Barely. To add credibility to my opinion. "All I had to do last week was let them think they'd beat us and we'd rolled over and played dead. And then."

Two shallow gulps that I swallowed hurriedly, appreciating the sensation of alcohol diluting my adrenaline.

"And then, bam! Friday night. Pull the plug on them. All I had to do was sit there and wait for one phone call from our guys in Singapore to let me know I'd gotten what I wanted. And that was it. Lock up the market and let them choke on their own greed. Do not pass go. Do not collect two hundred dollars. Do not collect dollar fucking one. Do not—"

I stopped at the centre of a breath, never fully drawing it for the next word.

I was doing it again.

The sudden realization caused my heartbeat to accelerate wildly as if I were fleeing from the recognition. I shook my head loosely, inhaled deeply, and tried to exhale as slowly as possible to disperse the fluttering in my chest.

Why did I keep doing it?

Talking to Judith.

3

T uesday morning.

Intermittent flecks of snow driven across the chalky February morning; but mostly dust and grit from the salted streets carried by the biting wind off Lake Ontario as it streamed down the canyons between the office towers in Toronto's financial district.

Twenty minutes after nine if you worked out your day in a single time zone; the day continuing without beginning or end, this side of the world or the other side, for myself and others who laboured in the global financial markets.

The sidewalks thinned by the wind-chill and final curtain of rush hour. I trudged across the concrete plaza between the office towers of the Toronto Dominion Centre. Despite running late, I persevered with my morning ritual of taking the stairs from the underground parking lot into the lobby of the tower opposite my office, and then walking outdoors across the plaza to my building, rather than flashing up in the elevator directly from my car to my office suite.

The controlled environments within the sealed glass office towers precluded me from touching the true rhythms of the day. Inside, I would be muffled by stale heat, re-chilled air, false, fluorescent light; insulated by my synthetic manipulation of money from an immense distance through computer impulse and intangible telephone words; never meeting the people I was dealing with or seeing the money I was trading. Without this exposure to a legitimate atmosphere, it was easier for me to get swept along in the frantic momentum of the markets; it was easier for my world, always seductive, always urgent, to lie to me.

The stiff wind tugged at me. I squinted, tucked my chin, glanced to both sides as I walked, trying to keep my eyes shielded from the blasts of grit. Noticed that, with the exception of a single kamikaze bike courier and a handful of shivering smokers hugging the revolving doors, I was alone on the concrete squares of the plaza. To someone looking down from the upper floors of the towers, I must have seemed like some forgotten chess piece struggling to cross the wind-blown board after the game had already been abandoned.

In my final steps to the doors, I pulled the metallic cold through my nostrils sharply. Searching for the part of the air that was genuine.

၍၏

Michelle, our receptionist, shaggy blonde bangs, her thirties nearly spent and her excessive weight haplessly cloaked in a pleated top, looked up from her computer keyboard through blue-rimmed designer bifocals and broke into a cheerful smile. Huge hoop earrings dancing against her round apple face, she reached to a shelf at the side of her station where snapshots of her cat and her nieces clung with yellowing Scotch tape, and lifted a clutch of pink message slips. "Morning, morning, morning. These are all for you from yesterday."

She bunched her florid cheeks into a conspiratorial grin and whispered a warning. "You-know-who is looking for you. And he's pissed. He's been bellowing around here for the last half hour."

I grinned back at her. Cardinal rule of deal-making: be nice to the receptionists and secretaries because they were the gate-keepers who got you in the door and they always knew the gossip and the score. But I also had a special relationship with Michelle, garnered from having her work late over the past several months to run the mountains of word processing from an unruly stack of contracts that always required urgent overnight revision for sending back to Singapore. Slugging it out four or five hours after closing to process the endless email between our attorneys and the Singapore attorneys, she had become close enough to be trusted without being so close that she was a threat.

I shrugged. "What else is new?"

"One more week until my vacation starts is what's new."

"And you have something sinful planned, I hope."

"Next weekend my girlfriend and I fly to Miami and hit that cruise ship. And we're gonna go wild."

I played along, made a face of scandalized goofiness. "I'll watch for the coverage on CNN."

That brought a giggle from her, a puff of glee that melted as soon as it hit the air.

On its tender ripple, I launched myself past her.

Several times at the weary finish of our late evenings I had taken her to dinner in appreciation of her dogged commitment. Each time I had carried away a sadness that would not wash away from how fiercely she generated her cheerfulness over margaritas, telling of evenings soaked up with watching her favourite television programs, talking on the phone for hours to her girlfriends. And then also her oblique references to nights when she had gone home with men, knowing they would never stay an extra hour or call the next day. Listening to her, I had felt in her voice how their silence settled on her like cold rain, and I had struggled to conceal my artless pity for how hurtful it must be for her to live in the loneliness left over from men who rejected her because she was overweight. That sadness, safely arms-length from my own, was one of the few emotions I had allowed myself to trust, let myself feel. Now, every time I saw her, I felt guilty that, beneath my listening to her dinner chatter, I had borrowed her emotions, spending them like some counterfeit currency to sustain myself through the gaps in my own life.

Walking, I stuffed the message slips in my pocket, shucked my overcoat, tossed it onto a chair through the open door of my office as I passed. Conserving my energy by avoiding the endless detours of catching up to telephone calls, faxes, and emails. Heading determinedly to the end of the hall, walking unannounced into the end office.

I paved my entrance with, "Morning, Kyle."

"Paris," Kyle acknowledged tightly. "Nice of you to show up."

"I was here until midnight most of last week. I needed a day to catch up. Left you a voice memo."

"I'm not talking about the hours."

"Neither am I."

"Don't I fuckin' know it." Dropping his reaction, unclothed by any qualification or pretence, into the several feet that separated us, was Kyle exercising his implicit licence of senior partner. Politeness reserved for valuable clients; competence our focus here. Kyle bounced his pen against a sheaf of loose correspondence and computer reports fanned across his desk. Chafing.

I fingered Kyle's favourite tactic: launch an uncomfortable and expectant silence, then seek to gain advantage by out-waiting me so any comment or explanation I offered could be immediately attacked and criticized.

I held back, letting the mounting seconds worm into him.

I watched him slide forward in his chair to close the distance between us; his lips pulled tight, the sparse grey wires of hair brushed against his receded hairline. I began to feel pinched in by his aggression.

In the grinding stillness, I studied Kyle warily, hoping to pluck some leverage for my defence from any careless body language; yet I was unable to come up with anything except, as usual, how poorly his suit jacket puckered around his shoulders and elbows. I was reminded that Kyle, staring down sixty, pumped weights for an hour a day at his health club with a personal trainer kept on the firm's payroll; regularly competing in the masters division of power-lifting contests even though he was often the shortest man at any business meeting or conference table. The lone un-retired founding partner of the firm, his authority and his emotional intensity, like his physical prowess, were lumped in his bulky upper body. His business and political power was hoarded in an untidy Rolodex, daubed and dog-eared and mulishly pre-served in an age of computer databases, guarding a hefty ros-ter of influential people he had accumulated and cultivated over several decades.

Under Kyle's fixed and unblinking stare, I made a display of leaning in the doorway casually, knowing from experience that much of my own competence emanated from projecting an illu-sion that I possessed a limitless reservoir of confidence.

Kyle broke first. "Where the hell were you when everything started to hit the fan yesterday?"

I stepped sideways, deflecting his words, settled into an arm-chair for effect. "I was three days ahead of it."

"How?"

"I started the whole party rolling in Singapore and Bangkok Friday night before I went home for the weekend."

"Why?"

"Why do you think?"

"No," Kyle insisted. "Why now?"

"Because the deal was completed a week ago. A month ago. There was no need to do anything more. No need to wait any longer."

"You start this deal over six months ago, then you miss half the meetings and let the deal stall until a month ago. Now you suddenly decide you're going to jump back in and the deal can't wait another month."

"I should have let it fail?"

"You should have waited."

My instincts warned me not to respond and risk being towed into the current of Kyle's antagonism.

Kyle tightened his elbows into his sides. Loading for punches. "Do you know the drain on our treasury position yesterday?"

"I can guess."

"Are you sure you can guess that big?"

"Then you tell me."

"Our treasury department's been flooded all night with emails and SWIFT messages from Bangkok Commercial Bank requesting settlement on the bond issue no later than March tenth. That's three weeks. How much do we need?"

I leaned forward to demonstrate that I was immune. "Come on, Kyle. Don't act like some cop came out of a speed trap and surprised you with a traffic ticket. You know that this Bangkok Commercial Bank deal has been our primary focus for the last couple of weeks. We've gone through ten meetings on strategy, hundreds of hours of crunching the numbers and working out the margins."

"How much of the bond issue did you buy?"

"More than expected."

"How much?"

"The whole issue."

"So, Paris, you're telling me we need a hundred million?"

"I'm telling you we need a hundred million."

"And we don't have the cash."

"But we've got a lot of it."

"How much?"

"A lot more than you think we have."

"How much is that?"

"Most of it from a single deal I put together in Singapore. And I think I can pull together a syndicate of a few more smaller players in Singapore and Hong Kong for the rest."

"No. How fucking much?"

"I don't know yet."

"Then you've just bankrupted this firm. We close our doors in less than a month."

"We—"

"Get out. Get the fuck out. Just get the fuck out."

I made a performance of drawing a breath, exhaling in overly tried patience; articulating that I was winning because Kyle was losing his temper.

"Before I went to Bangkok," I announced conspicuously, "we agreed I was going to run with this one." I opened my palms, concentrated on sprinting ahead of Kyle's next outburst. "When I came back from Bangkok—"

"That wasn't—"

"And reported on the preliminary negotiations, we agreed to run hard with it."

"What we planned—"

"And I have."

"That's an understatement! Paris, we talked buying on a best-efforts basis. About paying maybe twenty million, tops. From our own capital. And dialling for dollars to syndicate another twenty or thirty million. But only taking what we could pay for or pre-sell in syndication. Not a penny more."

"And paying for the rest of the offering by using the financing from Singapore."

"Agreed. You were supposed to be bringing on Bank of South Asia in Singapore to back us up with the additional mezzanine financing."

"Which I have."

"But we were going to broker the deal. Not buy it outright. We didn't expect to buy the entire bond issue and have to pay for the whole damn thing sight unseen. Now we're expected to settle up on a hundred million with Bangkok Commercial Bank. By March fuckin' tenth."

I waited.

In the diameters of discord and uneasy quiet that persisted between us, it seemed that we were breathing in unison. To break the grip of Kyle's anger and accusation I found myself expanding my chest and holding my lungs full.

"Paris, our treasury people are fielding all kinds of flack about where do we expect to get that kind of capital. Even if we sold off everything we owned in a fire sale, and leveraged that right to the hilt, we could barely raise half that much. Am I missing something? Was I not listening when you told me about how some rich uncle just died last week and left you a spare hundred million?"

I measured Kyle's rhythm, tried to interrupt it at a weak link. "That's not the important thing this minute."

"If it's not, I'd sure as hell like to know what is."

"The important thing is that we got the entire issue with no competition and no interference. And because we cut the competition out of the market, we got the deal at a much better price. A lot more profit for us. That's the important point."

"Except now we can't pay for it." Kyle hesitated. Sniffed savagely. "And that's the sure-as-shit important point!"

I listened to the heat pumping into the room and to the wind scouring the wide windows. Over Kyle's shoulder the city skyline wobbled in the ashen winter light.

Kyle struck swiftly, lowering his voice, levelling his tone, thrusting the allegation in his words. "You've been on shaky ground this past half year. Since ..."

"Since what?"

"Since you damn well know what."

"Let's," I stated, "keep my personal life out of this."

"Okay then," Kyle conceded in lemon tones, "let's keep it to your performance around here."

"Where the numbers speak for themselves."

"Sure. On your own you've produced as much income for the firm as the rest of us combined."

This was familiar between us; we recited our responses as if reprising them from previous dissonance.

"That's right," I said.

"But I built this firm with a team of partners," Kyle proclaimed. "Not with lone players."

"Yeah. Well. Fine." Giving ground would only give him momentum.

"I'm sure the directors would be interested in having their newest executive vice-president give them that fuck-you attitude at the next board meeting."

This was sour. And suspicious. Kyle gathering fuel from as many sources as possible to ensure that his accusations consumed everything in their path.

I refused Kyle sufficient quarrel, or voice, to let it go any further.

Scooping up the silence, Kyle regrouped, resumed his original censure. "You bring this deal to us last summer, sell us on your promise to pull if off, and then you miss half the meetings, missed half of everything around here, once we take it on."

This was a portent. Kyle resuming the course of least resistance. Refusing to concede the possibility of success for the bond sales, leaving me with the minimal defence of trying to brush aside the potential for failure. Seeking to lay the predicament at my feet in his indictment of my consistency, if not my competence. It was unsafe to remain in the path of such determination. Kyle had already choreographed this entire meeting in his mind ahead of time. There was no use trying to change any of it now. If I was lured into trying, I would be absorbed into his agenda. Better to cut it off. Get out.

"I missed those meetings for a reason," I told Kyle succinctly. "You know why. You saw it then. You just don't want to see it now."

It was a weak statement that I didn't feel entitled to truly believe. But it served. I watched Kyle's face slowly fill with coppery indignation, spreading from his nose out across his cheeks towards his temples.

"If you don't want to," I added, losing momentum, "I can't make you."

That was the end of it. We had both circled our conflicts long enough, talking around them to purposely ignore each other's points. Neither of us owned any progress. Neither could be bothered with any further arguing. Both of us were equally betrayed by it.

"Get out," Kyle grumbled blandly.

As much as I wanted to stand, pivot, and leave without another word, let Kyle re-breathe the staleness of his own aggression, I needed Kyle's cooperation. I needed the firm. I needed its capital and resources to ensure the success of my bonds. Let myself be reduced to striking back in similar rage and I would dilute the mortar necessary to join my deal and my career, to mend my life with fresh momentum.

Ducking his disregard, I tried to purge my tone of any admission or apology. "Give me a chance to make a few calls and check my faxes and email. And double-check our financing arrangements in Singapore overnight. It'll take the best part of twenty-four hours. We might as well put the exact numbers on the table. First thing tomorrow morning."

"We might as well, Paris."

Kyle was dismissing me; making it apparent that, in his opinion, I had lost the argument, if not something more.

As I turned, he caught me between the shoulder blades with a parting thrust. "If you had bothered to come to the office yesterday we wouldn't have to waste time waiting for this information now. Would we?"

Another of Kyle's perfected tactics, reducing the conflict to a personal criticism and leaving you with two losing choices: strike back and stray from the real issue; or stick to the issue and let the criticism stand undefended, making it valid, and making you pay a price in frustration and bile whenever he dredged it up against you in a future confrontation.

Doubly angered, I was tempted to collect on past debts. But this morning was not other mornings. My reserve of confidence was meagre, and I cautioned myself against squandering it by engaging in a retort.

Without response, I walked out, back to my office.

Why hadn't Kyle already gone storming to the board of directors? I had to ask myself. Why was he holding back?

There was more threat lurking in what he had not done than

in anything he could have done by denouncing me to the board before I could defend myself.

Twice along the hallway, I touched the walls with my finger-tips, unsure whether I was steadying myself or merely testing my connection with something solid.

や〇

In my office, I closed the door. Pulled the creased message slips from my pocket and flipped them to a corner of my desk. Sat motionless.

I refused to look at the calendars on my desk and computer. I had become afraid of the dates, afraid of their measuring of my life. I feared that I had already lived too long, experienced too much, used up my luck and all of my chances.

I tried to concentrate on suppressing the uncertainty that seeped into my thoughts from some deeper place within me.

In my mind I saw myself sitting out yesterday morning next to the electric kettle in my kitchen, its white plastic shell, cracked behind the spout, leaking steam for months, my shopping for a replacement lost within my overall procrastination one weekend to the next. There would never be a language affluent enough for me to explain it in words spoken aloud to another person: how not leaving my apartment had been necessity rather than choice.

I had woke in an unfamiliar bending of space and shadow in the false light before dawn, feeling as if I had been dug out of sleep by a blunt shovel.

In a stale bathrobe, I prowled the clamorous silence of my empty rooms. Sick. Unsteady after a murderous night of mur-derous dreams that had all been rinsed away at that exact second my eyes fluttered open, leaving me with ragged effigies of the dense emotion and confusion. I chased the fading dream images, stretching to heal myself by somehow linking the broken ends of my feelings to the raw ends of my broken-off dreams.

My concentration absent, my hands unguided, I fell into familiar routine. Fussing to fill and plug the kettle, spooning ground coffee into the glass carafe with the plunger. Pouring the boiling water. And then pouring the coffee. Inhaling the fragrant gush of steam from the mug.

It was not until I had lifted the mug and sipped that I noticed the second steaming mug still waiting on the kitchen counter.

I could not prevent myself from glancing to the hallway leading from the bedroom. Like grabbing at empty air halfway through an unexpected fall. I could not stop myself from expecting her to come shuffling into the kitchen.

Parked, then, at my kitchen table over slowly cooling bitter coffee, without her, I could think of nothing but all of the things now undone between us, all of the things we would now never share, our lives forcibly unravelled by a specific minute in time. I seemed to breathe by having to remember how to do it.

Breaking dawn brought a ferocious sun, shooting blindingly through the floor-to-ceiling windows; diffusing all the angles in the rooms and corners and hallways. Their shadows bleached away, the straight lines melted back into the walls.

How was I to navigate with no exact points of reference?

Anxiety swirled in my blood, bringing a headache that was too stubborn to either bloom or depart.

Even as I willed myself to remain motionless and tried to pierce the thick light by tightening my focus, the blurred lines along the ceilings and baseboards, and the dispersed angles in the corners of the room, refused to grant any purchase of motion or retreat from my thoughts and memories.

I saw our mornings, heard the growing silences between us. Felt the lost chances slip away.

I could not hide from pieces of life lived so deeply.

Nor were there any points of reference to plot my escape into the future.

Sitting at my kitchen table, hoarding my heartache, trying to write on the tabletop with my dripping coffee spoon in blotting letters "love has gone."

The voice within me ran ahead of the pokey scratchings of my spoon, demanding:

What was my life any more?

What would it mean after I died?

Where would they go, all of my thoughts and feelings?

How long would it last, death?

Unable to move.

Unable to function.

By noon, sunlight surged over me like high tide. The rooms and hallways poured out into window-glass reflections and mirrors and confused soft shimmerings at the edge of my vision where there should have been clarity. In the glare, my vision receded, leaving me trapped in a brain soup of distortion, weakened by sorrow.

In ribbons of regret streaming from my fingertips, the day spun itself out.

∽∾

Mid-afternoon. Only halfway down the river.

Despite remaining at my desk and computer keyboard through lunch to weed through my faxes, sow a handful of phone calls, and punch out new email, I had not produced the critical information needed to liberate the firm from the hundred-million-dollar payment it would have to make three weeks out. Singapore and Bangkok still asleep. With their information not yet available, I had only been able to work with a few stray calculations, recording the limited number of bond subscriptions booked from Toronto. Grabbing up their dollars like lifeboats and stringing them together where, at the bottom of my screen, they always sank under the immense load of the hundred-million-dollar bond payment.

For the last hour I had done little more than debate whether I could afford to escape the office on the pretence of going out to grab a sandwich if it meant Kyle or others might intercept negative information in messages returned to me before I had a chance to edit them.

What happened, instead, was that Michelle came to see me, hovering hesitantly just inside my office as if uneasy at being removed from the reception area.

"Mr. Smith. I always have coffee with Molly, Kyle Addison's secretary. She says that Mr. Addison says that the firm's in big trouble. That you did something in China or somewhere that is going to cause the firm to go bankrupt. Is that true? I'm really worried. I'm afraid to go on vacation and come home to find out that I don't have a job anymore. I'm afraid I should try to cancel the cruise and get some of my money back if I'm going to lose my job. I haven't got very much saved right now."

I was bluntly reminded of how my actions, however high they soared above daily routines and however measured, spilled into the lives of others. A sobering sense of obligation swelled within me. "No, sit down. I'll try to explain."

She entered, perching her thick hips delicately on the edge of a chair in front of my desk.

"First of all, let's begin at the beginning. You've been around here a year or so. Long enough to know how Kyle is. Haven't you?"

Obviously fearful of endangering herself with any gesture of overt disrespect, she shrugged lamely.

"Okay," I continued haphazardly, "suffice to say that over the last thirty years, Kyle's gotten so used to sitting in there under his Yale diploma like a bishop at high mass that he thinks God also graduated from Yale. And when he thinks anybody here in the firm has sinned, he wants the whole firm to know about it."

I watched her eyes drift; I was losing her in the residue of my own resentment.

"But that still doesn't explain anything to you, does it?"

"No."

"And that still doesn't make your vacation any easier, does it?"

She shook her head.

I inhaled slowly, collected my thoughts. "The reason Kyle is storming around here this morning is because I committed the firm to buy up an entire bond issue in Bangkok. And we have to pay for it within a month. And Kyle's convinced we haven't got the cash. So he's screaming that it's going to drive the firm into bankruptcy."

"Is this from all the work I did for you a couple of months ago?"

"That's right."

"Are we? At risk of going bankrupt?"

"I've pre-sold a lot of the bonds in syndication."

She bit her lip. "I haven't told anyone else. In January I started the level-one securities course on Thursday nights."

"Good for you."

"You always made it sound so interesting when I was doing that work." She quickly added, "We haven't got to syndications. Only stocks."

"Okay. If stock is ownership of a piece of equity in a company, a bond is an IOU from the company. I borrow ten dollars from you. I promise to pay you back at the end of the month. I promise to pay you a dollar in interest. I write you an IOU that says I will pay you eleven dollars at the end of the month."

She brightly contributed a piece from her coursework. "But there's also secondary trading in stocks and bonds."

"Right. You can wait until the end of the month, present my IOU, and demand eleven dollars payment. Or you can sell the IOU to someone else in the middle of the month for ten and a half dollars, take the money, and run."

"Which is an over-the-counter trade."

"Exactly. The next phase in financial engineering, after trading, is syndication. In syndication, instead of selling the bonds after they're issued, we're the mandated agent and lead book-runner, and we pre-sell the bonds to syndication partners and other book-runners before they're issued."

Her eagerness faded. I had lost her in technical terms. And she was embarrassed to admit it. I kicked myself. I wanted to be generous. I wanted to reimburse her for the emotions I had covertly borrowed from her, and to try, however inadequately, to compensate her for the silence of unseen men who had dismissed her as unworthy of attention.

"That's okay," I assured her. "You ever had a yard sale?"

"Sure."

"So suppose your neighbour was going to have a yard sale a week from now and you looked over into his back yard at all the stuff he was going to sell next week. And you thought it looked like a lot a valuable stuff. So you offered to buy the whole lot of it for five hundred dollars."

"Okay."

"Except you won't pay him until next Saturday, until the actual day that he has scheduled for the yard sale. Okay?"

"If you say so."

"Then you go and take pictures of everything in the yard. And all week you go around to all of your friends. You show them pictures of all of the yard sale stuff. And you sell them all the stuff from the pictures. So far so good?"

"So far."

"Okay. Now next Saturday, all of your friends come over to your house and they pay you for everything. And all of the money they pay you adds up to six hundred dollars. And you turn around and walk over to your neighbour and you pay him the five hundred dollars you owe him for the stuff. Then you hand the stuff over to your friends who you've pre-sold it to."

I noticed the twitch of irritation from my words in the mirror of her face. I sounded patronizing. In my seclusion, my faculty to touch others has been buried beyond reach. I rushed to wrap up by dropping my palms open. "Then, what are you left with? Even though all the stuff is gone and even though you paid five hundred dollars to your neighbour for the stuff? How much is your profit?"

"A hundred dollars."

"That's what pre-selling a bond issue in syndication is like. Right now I'm running around selling the bonds before they're issued. And when it comes time to pay for the bonds, I'll have all the money from the syndicate partners who've subscribed to them."

"And you'll have a profit?"

"Welcome to Dodge City where every two-bit stock salesman wants to become a financial syndications gunslinger."

She dropped our eye contact, not knowing how to respond to slang that was familiar to me, foreign to her.

To compensate, I offered, "I'll be glad to help you with your course any time you want."

"Thank you. I'd appreciate that. Just don't mention it, okay. The other girls will gossip if they think I'm trying to get ahead of them."

She raised her eyes, hesitated.

"Does this," I asked, "make you feel any better about going on vacation?"

"Is this what you'll be doing when I'm on vacation?"

"Day and night."

She twisted up from her chair, then lingered before leaving. "Mr. Smith?"

"Yeah."

"Is this what you really do around here?"

I nodded. "Just like yard sales. Except the money has more zeros."

My attempted levity did not register. Deflecting back off her poorly concealed doubt, my words settled heavily, like layers of sand being poured around my ankles.

"Don't worry," I tried to reassure her in rapidly spun syllables. "I've got a secret weapon that's not available in yard sales."

"What?"

"I've got Stanley Man."

Puzzled, she scratched her wrist and quietly walked out. Leaving me saddened for having tried. Leaving me irritated that she has made me feel responsible for eroding her happiness.

Was there anyone left I had not in some way failed?

In my world, sometimes, progress was measured in proximity to power and consent rather than financial profit and loss.

In the final remnants of the afternoon, Kyle appeared in my office doorway—a concession of coming, unannounced and informally, several dozen feet down the corridor to me rather than summoning me back to his office to resume the morning's arguing.

"Sit down," I offered. Two steps backward when accusations boiled, one step forward when they simmered back down.

"How're we doing? What's the count?" Kyle inquired, dropping into a chair, his voice now deflated by a day laden with unabated apprehension.

I kept my shrug neutral. I had no emotional stamina for further confrontation. Any more, even the least confrontation stirred up a sickening feeling like anticipating the menace of a blindside blow.

"Like I said, Kyle, it's still going to take a couple more hours until the sun comes up on the other side of the world. I'll be here late talking to them. Like all last week. I'll stay on it. And it's not as if we have to make a deadline today. We've got three weeks. I built a couple of weeks extra margin into it."

Kyle chewed at the inner pocket of his cheek. "I'm still worried as hell about the cash."

"I'll bring the commitments in."

"From whom?"

"Bank of South Asia."

"How?"

"Most of the negotiations are complete."

"Will we have enough?"

"We'll have enough."

"Paying for the whole issue still worries the shit out me."

"We both know how important it is for everyone to see us paying for those bonds without having to scramble."

"Scrambling may not be our only problem."

Kyle's contention left several seconds of icy silence between us.

In tepid tones, I tried to curve the conversation around our dilemma. "Underneath all our posturing with Bangkok Commercial, we both know the really important thing is that we bought the entire issue with no interference. We own it. We beat out Amsterdam Bank. We beat out a bank a hundred times bigger than us."

I abandoned the words I was speaking. Raced ahead to evaluate my next statements.

Sidestepping all references to our shortfall of funds, I tried to stack up our advantages to avert Kyle's forecasts of collective hazard. "I planned it. I put it in motion. And then I made that whole Amsterdam crew think that we'd rolled over and died so that the greedy bastards would keep pre-selling the entire bond issue until they'd over-subscribed it two or three times."

"Amsterdam Bank can do that," Kyle granted in small accord. "Like you say, they've got a thousand times our capital. And a hundred times more salesmen to sell off the bonds."

"And that's their usual style, isn't it?"

"Of course it's their style, Paris. When they want a bond issue, they come in with unlimited amounts of cash to buy it up. And then they resell it before they've even paid for it."

"And they make a killing in the profit spread."

"Of course. That's the whole idea."

"And they beat the shit out of small investment banking firms like us every time."

Kyle nodded. "Well, what else are we supposed to do when we don't have the capital behind us. Like right now?"

"That's right. We always get nothing. If we're good boys and suck up nicely maybe they throw us a few crumbs. But only at their jacked-up secondary pricing. So our profit barely covers our costs of making the sale. And we always convince ourselves that's okay because we're making a name for ourselves in the international markets and we're at least paying overheads while we're doing it."

"Well, that's the way it is when we're limited by not having any retail deposit base."

"Yeah, and what else do big banks like Amsterdam Bank always do?"

Purposefully, I waited, making Kyle reduce the pace of his suspicion and reproach.

"Is that a rhetorical question? Or do you really want to waste time discussing it when we've got this other mess staring us in the face right now?"

From the flare of frustration in Kyle's voice, and the slicing gestures of his open hands, I knew I was pawning myself to certain failure if I let Kyle bully me from my rationale and validation. I struggled to tether him to my reasoning, running down my points.

"No. It's important. What Amsterdam Bank does as soon as they've got the entire bond issue oversubscribed is go back to the bond issuer and beat the living shit out of them to lower the purchase pricing. And double their own in-house profits. And what choice does the poor bond issuer have. They have to cave in on pricing. Because they're guaranteed that the entire bond issue is already sold. And they're sitting there with visions of dollars dancing in their heads. They can't wait to get their hands on all the cash. And there sits the Amsterdam Bank gang. Smiling across the boardroom table with a big bag of cash in their hands."

"Paris, I still don't know what all this has to do with us."

"We decided we were going to Bangkok Commercial Bank and put in a bid for the bonds. Put in a bid against Amsterdam Bank."

"Right."

"And what did you think was going to happen? What did you really think was going to happen?"

"Probably that we'd get beat out."

"But maybe we'd get a little side action. Right?"

"Right."

"So here's how I worked it." I could feel myself sprinting to get it all out before he closed down. "As soon as Amsterdam Bank started to heat things up and throw their weight around with their big amounts of cash, I retracted our bid."

"You retracted our bid?"

"Right."

"No," Kyle corrected imperatively. "That takes a full vote from the board of directors."

"Most bids, yes. But not this bid. There was a retraction clause included in the bid when we approved it and signed it to submit to Bangkok Commercial Bank. To make sure we had a trapdoor out of the deal if we needed one."

Kyle ploughed at the carpet with his heels. "So?"

His response, curt and cutting. The meanness of the meetings we conducted in private, where there were no witnesses to curb our incivility, our niggardly accommodation of one another.

I stiffened my confidence, spoke sternly and precisely, without pause for further breath, pressing the full accumulation of facts and consequences out at Kyle like a rude shove. "So. When I retracted our bid, I didn't let any of our clients know. I didn't let the markets know. I didn't let our salesmen know. But I made sure to leak the news to Amsterdam Bank. We made sure they knew in their Singapore office. And we even made sure they knew in Amsterdam. So Amsterdam Bank immediately assumed we had rolled over and died. And they went to market and sold the shit out of the issue."

"And?"

I concentrated on my words, finding it cumbersome to float the facts up into clearer waters above the sediments of doubt and confusion that dwelled within me.

"And then I just waited for them to go back to Bangkok Commercial Bank with their usual strong-arm tactics. That's were I spent all my time. Cultivating the directors of Bangkok Commercial. They were only too happy to let me know when Amsterdam Bank began to turn up the heat. Then I resubmitted our bid at the original price. Which was now a good deal higher than what Amsterdam Bank was offering to pay for the bonds. And Bangkok Commercial were only too happy to accept it."

"And what about Amsterdam Bank?"

"The directors of Bangkok Commercial Bank ruled to cancel them out of the deal for breach of contract. We blew Amsterdam right off the map."

"And what about Amsterdam Bank's pre-selling of those bonds?"

"You know as well as I do, Amsterdam's only got two choices right now."

"They've got no bonds to deliver."

"Damn right they've got no bonds to deliver. Because we own all of them. We own the entire issue."

"So Amsterdam Bank has to renege on delivery."

"Only two choices. They can renege on delivery and go around the markets with egg on their faces. Or they can come to us and buy all the bonds from us so that they have enough to fill their orders."

"And we'll be glad to sell them our bonds."

"At a profit, we'll be glad to sell them our bonds. At a hell of a profit."

Kyle frowned, squeezing his forehead and his chin into pouches and furrows, shook his head in discouraged appreciation of the facts. "They can't be happy. Amsterdam Bank."

"They're furious."

"And they'll come gunning for us, Paris."

"You and I both know they will."

"And how did you get Bangkok Commercial Bank to even reconsider our bid."

"I convinced them that we had most of the cash to pay for the entire issue."

"Which we don't have."

"But which we are borrowing."

"From whom?"

"From Bank of South Asia."

"What? You pledged the bonds as collateral for an asset-backed line of credit with Bank of South Asia?"

"Bet your ass. And I went to Bangkok Commercial and waved around the contract for the asset-backed credit line with Bank of South Asia that we had quietly pocketed."

"And now what?"

"Like you say, now we've got to pay for a hundred million dollars worth of bonds."

Kyle crossed over, letting his voice swell with gluey anxiety. "And we don't have the cash."

"But we've got the credit financing."

"Stop right there," Kyle warned. "What about this credit?"

I swallowed my surge of indignation. "What?"

"Anything else we don't know about?"

"No. Standard stuff."

"How standard?"

"Bank of South Asia lends us eighty per cent of the price of the bonds."

"Standard terms?"

"Yeah. We pre-pledge the bonds to BSA before we buy them. BSA lends us eighty cents on the dollar. We use the eighty million to pay most of the purchase price for the bonds. The rest we raise ourselves."

"We repay BSA on our sale of the bonds?"

"Right. We have to repay BSA in ninety days. When we sell the bonds into the open market, or to Amsterdam, whoever bids the most, cash is paid into escrow. BSA takes eighty cents of every dollar in escrow to retire their loan, then they release the bonds at the end of ninety days for settlement of the sale."

He refused to acknowledge that the credit arrangements were ordinary, using his silence to pry under my facts suspiciously.

To retaliate, I slipped back into the tone lingering from my discussion with Michelle. "We pledge the bonds. They lend us eighty per cent of the purchase price. We pay back when we sell the bonds."

Kyle cast me off with disdain. Flicking his fingers. "Yeah. Brilliant."

I could feel his doubt working, like cold water dripping.

"Have we locked up the eighty million from BSA?" he inquired sharply.

"Of course."

"Okay, BSA lends us most of the money we need to buy the bonds. So we can turn around and resell them right quick before the interest on the BSA loan sneaks up and bites us in the ass. Where's the rest of it? The discount settlement is ninety-two. Where's the other twelve or so million we still need?"

"I can pull together a syndicate of a few smaller players in Singapore for most of the rest."

"Then tell me. Right now. In plain clear English. Just how much we've raised so far."

"It's still going to be a few more hours until..."

"To the penny!"

Kyle planted his rage around him like fence posts.

I was reminded that this was also about our previous arguments that had ended inadequately; they had been accumulating over the last several months; vigorously chewed but never swallowed.

With Kyle slipping over the edge into a predictable free-fall of fear and anger, I recognized for a second time in the day that my failure and frustration were assured if I made the mistake of continued discussion and was lured into the trap of assuming Kyle was heading towards principled debate.

"A few more hours," I announced, wrapping it up quickly. "Until the markets open in Asia and I can call a few people and get some email back."

"I don't trust it," Kyle stated, tapering off into sullen silence.

That, I recognized, was Kyle postmarking his control of the situation. If everything worked out smoothly, his comments would be discarded. But if anything went wrong, he would have this exact point of reference to prove that he had been in command, able to verify that he had warned against it and that nothing had slipped by him.

"I don't trust it," he repeated as he stood. "And I don't trust you on it."

He walked out.

When did you ever?

4

At night I repeatedly woke from sleep exhausted from re-dreaming old dreams.

I felt as if I had no new dreams.

Every night I felt as if I were trapped in a backwash of sleep with the same images tumbling in on me. Nothing but re-runs out of the shadows. Leaving me barren when I woke.

My dreams were overused memories of dreams I had dreamed before; as if nothing new was happening within me emotionally, within my experiencing of life.

So there was nothing new to draw upon.

Nothing new to dream about.

Living on leftovers.

5

In February, in the city, winter lopped off the afternoon at its knees.

Within our offices, the intensity of the fluorescent light neither wavered nor dimmed. You would only notice the change outside in snapshots when you looked up between telephone calls or looked off your computer screen. First the deepening mid-afternoon shadows shouldered along the canyons between the office towers. Then it was black outside the windows, without further increment, as if the blackness spilled down from the sky.

Often you could hear the end of the day in the rising volume of vehicle horns barking in rush-hour before you took notice of the gloom, punctuated by streetlights, pierced by headlights and checkered by distant shoals of lit up high-rise windows.

Soothed by the cliffs of familiar darkness outside my windows, I sat patiently in my office, my apprehension easing as I listened to voices disappearing into the elevators, the expanding emptiness of the office leaving me insulated from interruption or reproach. I flipped through a wad of yellow computer slips confirming the day's string of bond trades. My eyes retraced packs of numbers and decimal points that dissolved within my concentration without registering any meaningful information. I brushed the bundle aside.

My confrontation with Kyle came back on me like heartburn. I hated it, how it had gone. I hated how Kyle had withdrawn his support this past year and made me a target because I had elevated my commitment to my personal life above my commitment to the firm. I had tried to make caring about someone the most important thing in my life, certain that it would make me invincible; and, instead, it had left me on the outside of potent office alliances, compromised and vulnerable. It left me feeling as if I had been betrayed by something I could not see or touch.

Listlessly, I slumped in my chair, leafing through a two-month-old copy of *Forbes* magazine to keep my hands busy while I waited for it to be time to make the call.

Often, when I was about to call to the other side of the world, I imagined the sun rolling freshly through the streets of a foreign city; the recipient of my call rising from slumber, preparing for the day in morning rituals similar to my own, travelling to work along hectic streets banked by gaudy advertising.

Memories of my last trip to Singapore broke my clouded thoughts: cleanly swept streets and lush parks planted with palms and broad-leafed tropical plants; gleaming office towers looking out over the green sea and verdant islands of Indonesia; on the streets, heat and steamy humidity doubling the weight of the air in your lungs; and then the chill of the air conditioning, bringing welcome relief as it soaked slowly back into your shirt when you got off the elevator heading for someone's office.

I clicked my mouse, and brought my database of names and addresses up onto the screen, not trusting myself to dial the twelve digits from memory.

My call to Bank of South Asia was answered on the second ring by a woman chirping heavily accented English.

I asked for Stanley Man by his full Mandarin name, properly placing the family name first.

"Man Sek-Lung, please."

"Who is calling, please?"

"Paris Smith. Addison, Beaufort and Shulman. Toronto. Canada."

"One moment, please."

There was a pause unusual to the frenetic pace of Asian business.

"Hello. Mr. Smith, are you still there? I'm giving you a forwarding number for Mr. Man."

"What do you mean, a forwarding number?"

"Please contact Mr. Man at the following number."

She slowly announced a number that I realized, as I double-checked it against my computer screen, was Stanley's home telephone number. I re-dialled quickly, nervously.

The telephone was not answered until the fifth ring.

"Stanley?"

"Yes."

"Paris Smith. What's up? You taking the day off?"

"Not quite, I'm afraid."

"What do you mean?"

"The bank and I parted company Friday night, Paris. Actually, I was called in and let go."

"Stanley. Shit. Were you expecting anything?"

"I suppose it's been in the wind the last couple months. But I thought the timing would be a lot different."

"You come out of it okay?"

"Better than I thought. They could have gone with a severance package as low as three months' salary. I was hoping for six. They gave me twelve. And I've been keeping a few options open in Singapore and Hong Kong, and one in Beijing. So I'm in great shape."

"Glad to hear that. But who takes over the file for Bangkok Commercial Bank to run with our deal now?"

"Well, Paris, that's the part that's not in great shape."

"What do you mean?"

"In short... there is no deal."

"Don't tell me that."

"I've got nothing else to tell you. The deal is dead."

"And don't tell me that either."

"Paris, that deal is deader than my job. That's the whole reason I got the axe."

"I don't understand. You and I designed that credit line to guarantee some very high fees to BSA. It'll probably be the richest deal BSA does this year."

"Except there is no deal. It's off. The deal is dead."

"The deal can't be dead. You can't cancel a done deal. There's six and a half pounds of contracts."

"And that's the problem."

"What?"

"There are no more contracts, Paris."

"What do you mean? You can't just cancel out all those contracts or throw them away. We'd sue BSA for breach. Hell, we wouldn't even have to sue. We'd just have to go through the motions so that the story spreads around. Nobody would ever get into bed with BSA again. And somebody else would step up to marry us at the altar as soon as it got out how rich the deal was. Hell, for that much profit we'd probably hear from Credit Lyonnais or Barclays or JP Morgan Chase."

"That's just it. BSA won't be in breach of contract, and they won't be walking away from the contracts."

"What then?"

"They sold the contracts."

"Sold them?"

"They had to."

"How? How can you sell a contract? And who did you sell it to?"

"I'm not exactly sure how. But I know why. And I know who."

"Well, then, who?"

"Amsterdam Bank."

"Amsterdam Bank? No fucking way either of us would ever deal with them. We put this whole bond deal together to screw Amsterdam Bank. How could they even get into the game, how could they even get into the ball park, let alone get into the deal?"

"You want the short version, Paris? Or do you want the long details?"

"Give me the short version."

"Amsterdam Bank sent someone in to BSA. They let it be known that they own the controlling share of half a dozen insurance companies across the Pacific Rim. And between them, all of these insurance companies hold one awful shit-load of Bank of South Asia stock in the Hong Kong, Singapore, and Australian stock markets."

"And?"

"And they threatened to start dumping all of the stock unless they become a partner in the deal."

"And BSA caved in to that?"

"Hey, BSA took a couple of big hits in China and Vietnam and a few other places that over the last two years that have left it overexposed and under-capitalized. If those Amsterdam Bank insurance companies start dumping the stock, the share price will dive. As soon as the share price caves in, BSA's equity shrinks and it can't meet reserve requirements. Then the Bank of International Settlements steps in. Rumours trickle out into the capital markets. BSA is fucked. They can start turning the branches into hamburger stores."

"Amsterdam can't do it. They'd never get away with it."

"There's nothing to stop them. Think about it. It's not like dealing with a single company in a single stock market like London or New York where everyone lives in almighty fear of the regulators. It's a handful of different companies and half a dozen different stock markets. They're not afraid of anything except losing a couple of dollars worth of profit on their stocks. Which they'll just swap for shares in other bank stocks anyway."

"There's still probably some part of it that's against the law somewhere."

"And you and me, and everybody else in this business, know that when you're dealing with this much money on anything there is no law."

"For money? Amsterdam?"

"Of course not. You know they wanted to set an example. Stamp out this problem before it got started. Stamp out anyone else from ever thinking about trying again."

"Fuck."

"Amsterdam couldn't touch Bangkok Commercial for pulling the bonds out from under their feet. So they clobbered you guys."

"Who did Amsterdam Bank send in to see you guys."

"I don't know. I never saw or heard anything. I got it from the chairman and he had two of the directors with him. And they wouldn't answer anything for me."

"Why didn't they keep you around rather than let you loose with the information?"

"They wanted to. That's what the whole meeting was about.

They wanted me to keep running with the deal. They wanted me to work with Amsterdam Bank. But I refused. So they fired me. The year's severance is being paid in instalments, to keep a lid on me, but you and I both know there's really not much I can do to hurt either BSA or Amsterdam Bank other than one or two embarrassing stories that they can make go away pretty easily."

"If you refused out of loyalty, I appreciate it."

"Well, partially out of loyalty to you and your firm. Mostly because, sooner or later, everything I do for the rest of my career in this business will come down to my reputation for keeping my word."

"Thanks for that much anyway."

"Sorry, Paris."

"Will anybody at BSA give me more details?"

"They'll have to. Or their attorneys will have to. Try Albert Quan, the chairman. You've met him before. Worst he can do is refuse to talk to you."

"I guess so. Can I stay in touch with you at this number for a while or are you out to Hong Kong?"

"No, I'll be here. They made sure I didn't take anything out of my office. But I wiped my office computer clean into a couple of downloads, so they'll be missing a few of the private memos we shot back and forth to each other. And I've already got all of the documentation for the deal on the computer here at the house. There's a few internal memos on the Amsterdam angle, but nothing that will really stand up under light of day. I can always go through the files and see if I can find anything that might help."

"Thanks."

"Least I can do."

We stuffed a few personal comments into the conversation to

bring it to a rapid close, equally eager to cease feigning momentum that was no longer there, equally eager to flee the hovering stigma of personal failure. Then we hung up sharply.

Acid crept up my esophagus. I forced it back down in a smarting swallow. I drilled my eyes around my empty office. I was at first anxious, then confused as to why I was not more furious.

It was backwards.

My rage should have been absolute, my grip on it like my grip on a lethal weapon.

Instead, the more my rage compelled me to return to the ruthless facts from Singapore, the more I choked on my shame of failure.

There was no reassuring heat from the familiar surge of adrenaline that flowed invariably from a business crisis.

Instead, I had a sense of all of my other feelings going cold and watery. My vigour and confidence cowering. My hope hiding.

It left me with an aberrant sensation of being present in the passing moments, while also of living outside myself, of being detached and looking down on myself.

I crooked my toes compulsively within my shoes, searching for the solidity of the floor, my urge to flee so intense I sensed it would take no more than an uneven breath to send me into the corridor.

Was this what it was like for Judith? This absence of everything familiar?

Was this what made her do it?

I tried to move, pushing myself forward while keeping the brakes on so that I did not lurch or stumble.

To the door, to the corridor, to the elevator, to the street. I touched as little as possible with my fingers. I kept my eyes on my toes to prevent myself tripping. I arrived outside on the deserted flats of concrete in the dark cold air without any recollection of the stages of my passage, only a series of blurred images, like paint slopped on walls, sliding down.

I leaned into the chilled air for support.

Fever flared in the cavities of my brain, as if my blood was being scalded; it roared at my temples, straining to escape my skull.

Words bubbled up my throat and then flew off my lips like flushed birds before I could speak them.

I felt lost in my skin.

I craned my neck, looking up to the surrounding office towers, trying to see through the concrete and steel to the reassurance of lives continuing to be lived in those offices, but could only feel the immense weight of the money, indifferent to my plight. I was forced to peer farther out to the distant constellations in the night sky to situate myself so I would not be flung out by the dizzying rotation of the earth I felt coming up through the concrete beneath my shoes.

Bringing my eyes back to street level, one light beckoned: at the top of the block, a franchised coffee shop that stayed open twenty-four hours to pick up trade from the late-shift cabbies and office cleaning crews omnipresent throughout the midtown and financial district during the night.

I shivered, tugged my coat tighter at my throat, pulled in a string of burly breaths in an attempt to settle my jumpy breathing, and headed up the block in a long looping jay-walk.

I was exhausted beyond any familiar limit. Feeling as if my emotions had been beaten with sticks. I began to picture myself arriving home, going from the front door straight to the couch in the fewest possible steps and dropping fully clothed, deadly tired, into sleep.

I knew I was facing a terrible night and that it would be worse in the morning.

I knew, in my life, there was now something irreparably wrong.

I knew I had been waiting for it to happen.

The pool of light leaking from the shop out onto the dark street reminded me of shallow water. I waded into it, watchful of deep spots. I pushed through the door, entering into the brightness and the smell of coffee and doughnut grease. The place was empty. A skinny black girl in a moss-green T-shirt presided over the counter, reading a spread newspaper to the accompaniment of a reggae radio station, her hips shifting with the beat.

Without looking up, she asked, "You want coffee?"

I sat at a stool. "Yeah. Please."

She straightened from the counter and turned to the stewing carafes behind her. "Here or to go? Regular?"

"Here," I told her. "Regular's fine. Thanks."

Clicking; clinking; and she slid the mug onto the counter in front of me.

I took a sip.

To stay away from my memories of Monday morning, vaguely stirred into the sweet creamy taste, I asked her, "Is your accent from Jamaica?"

"No," she answered. "Trinidad."

"You're a long way from home."

"Long way from home. And cold as hell." She grinned. "Don't you know."

I replied with a nod and a tight smile, wanting her to know that I was grateful for her recognition of me.

"What 'bout you? You're surely no taxi man dressed like that. You one of them super stock market men?"

"Yeah," I admitted, "I guess I am."

"Then what you doin' down here at midnight? You not make enough millions today?"

I shrugged. "Just a hard night."

"That happens," she said. "Sometimes, man, the night comes hard."

I had to nod.

Don't you know.

6

The water ripples around her foot in gentle circles.

From one side of her foot, the circles disappear into shadows under the dock.

From the other side, the circles melt outward into the lake
where the water and the sun become the same brightness.

The afternoon seems without beginning or end.

I walk down to the dock, sipping on a cold sweating beer bottle,
bristles of sun-burnt grass stubble pricking my bare feet.

I am conscious of slowing my pace, taking shorter steps the
closer I get to the dock, so that I can keep watching her.

Stretched out on the dock, she is leaning back against an old
upturned wooden lawn chair. Bathing suit bottom. Baseball T-
shirt. Her hair stuffed under a faded canvas hat, strands falling
loose onto the flaking paint of the weather-cracked chair slats.

Reading her trashy paperback against one propped knee.

Her other knee bent over the side of the dock, her toes touching
the water, her foot making a lazy circle. Casting ripples outward.

When I step onto the dock, I stop.

The air is motionless and scorched, with the faint smell of road
dust and barbecue smoke and the algae on the rocks beneath the
dock.

Laughter and children's voices and the joyful yipping of a dog *drift through the trees from the next cottage. And radio music. Rock-and-roll songs.*

Feeling my weight on the boards, she glances up from her book. "What are you looking at?" she asks.

"You," I tell her.

"Why?"

"Because I love you."

"Why?"

"Because you're beautiful."

"Why?"

"Because you're you."

She smiles, lets her book slide. "Do you ever wonder why I love you?"

"Sometimes."

"Sometimes it's because you do things like talking me into getting out of the city for a few days. This old beat-up place with all the spider webs in the rafters. Our anniversary here."

I step to her.

I kneel down. I kiss her softly, her skin hot and salty with sweat.

"Be careful," she whispers. "You could kiss a girl right out of her pants like that."

"I was thinking more about making this last forever. Us. Having this afternoon together."

"That too," she whispers.

7

I could not recall any point previous to these last few days when I had ever before been intimidated by daylight.

Mid-morning, I flicked my eyes around my office hurriedly to check for any overlooked details that would salvage my situation, preparing to push myself from my chair.

Yellowish sunlight, diffused by the tinted glass of the broad windows, had leaked in around me.

I hated it, bloated with lemony brightness.

With no shadows, I felt denied any sense that there was something left unseen, something yet to discover, some new possibilities or solutions.

I was hatefully tired.

I had spent the night in a chair in my living room. Three times I had tried to reach Albert Quan; falling back into a tense and listless sleep, the lamp light seeping under my eyelids, each time the man would not take my call. The final time I woke it had been dawn. With the twelve-hour time difference, the business day in Singapore had run to its conclusion. Bank of South Asia had closed. My attempted contact incomplete. My possibilities shrinking.

At my desk, I swallowed sorely, my throat dry. My eyes scratchy with fatigue. Feeling forced to take on my business day, empty-handed and reluctant, as it unfolded in uncertainty and false glare.

Time to report to Kyle's called meeting.

I took a final breath, trying to disband my doubts. In unbroken momentum, I rocked to my feet, paced rapidly out of my office, down the hall, and through Kyle's open door.

There were four of them waiting: Kyle behind his desk; on two inward-facing chairs, Brenda Gibbons from our treasury department, Dimitri Sarkans from trading; and, on the deep couch along the side wall, an older man I did not recognize.

Kyle commenced while I was still entering the room. "Sit down, Paris. I've invited Brenda and Dimitri in to keep them informed of what's happening firsthand."

I nodded to them.

"And I'd like to introduce Ted Dwyer." Kyle swept his hand to the older man. "Ted and I go back a long way. All the way to Yale, in fact. At various times, Ted has been president of two of our largest brokerage houses and one of our largest banks. These days he spends most of his time up in Ottawa warming a bench in the Senate, but I persuaded him to fly down this morning to give us the benefit of some of his experience and perspective."

I stepped over and shook hands with Dwyer who, with difficulty, hiked himself partially out of the couch cushions, prefacing his greeting with, "Sorry. With this hip replacement, I always need a little more advance notice to get up and running."

I eyed the remaining chair.

Instinct warned me not to relinquish my command of the ground between Kyle and Dwyer.

"Okay." Kyle launched the discussion impulsively, like tearing the paper from a cheaply wrapped package. "Paris, what have you got for us? Our treasury department has a stack of overnight messages from Bangkok Commercial Bank requesting settlement on the bond issue no latter than March tenth. That's three weeks. How much do we have from Bank of South Asia?"

I stood before them.

I looked at their faces in sequence, all united with Kyle in their stares of doubt and indictment.

What to tell them? What not to?

(Was the raging in my ears what a diver felt while suspended in the drop with no return available to the anchored footing of the diving board? Did you consume the gravity in your descent, becoming calmer as you neared the crash with the water?)

"We may," I opened, "have a lot less than we need. But..."

Kyle wedged in his demand like a knife blade. "Less?"

"But we may not need anything at all."

"Why?"

"Because we may not have a deal at all."

"Bottom line," Kyle demanded, swift and severe.

I scrambled for some lean line of argument. "I got hold of Bank of South Asia last night. They're our financing arm for the deal. Suddenly there's a lot of confusion. Even though we're sitting with all their contracts in hand. They sound like they're trying to back out on us. From the looks of it, I think the whole deal is going to come unravelled. And we're not going to have any financing. But there aren't going to be any bonds available for us either. So we're not going to get any bonds, we're not going to owe anything. It's a wash. And we just move on to the next deal."

"No."

Halted by Ted Dwyer's pronouncement lobbed in from the side of the room, I stood, reticent, uncertain how to proceed, steeping in my own frustration.

Tall, thin, and balding, with thick folds of skin under his jaw where he had once been beefy, Ted leaned back into the couch, bunching the blazer bearing his thready air squadron crest on its pocket, and unceremoniously brushed a scattering of dandruff from his shoulders and lapels.

"We already know that this thing has blown up in your face," Ted stated. "But it seems we're not the only ones that know."

Sensing I would make myself vulnerable by having to ask for more details, I only raised my eyebrows in inquiry to Dwyer.

Adroitly, he handed me back off to Kyle with a curt nod.

"This," Kyle explained, lifting several sheets of paper from his desk with tangible disdain. "Waiting for me when I came in this morning. Faxed in to us from London just after their open. From Amsterdam Bank."

I could only wait for more.

"It's their offer, Paris. For the Bangkok Commercial Bank bonds. They'll give us eighty cents on the dollar for bonds that we buy for ninety-two cents on the dollar. If we take it we'll only lose twelve million."

"But there's no way—"

"And if we hustle around and do a lot of selling for them on the side they'll pay us enough commission that we can carve our loss down to ten million."

Kyle snapped the pages against his fingers.

Thinking there would be more, I waited in the ensuing silence while Kyle's words drifted down like dry, brittle leaves.

When no one else spoke up, I began constructing my protest. "We have contracts with Bangkok Commercial. And with BSA. That let us off the hook..."

"Apparently not."

"Amsterdam can't do that."

"Apparently, they have."

Again, from my periphery, Ted Dwyer's voice intruded, casual and terse.

"Amsterdam Bank not only knows this firm is in trouble. They know a great deal about how much trouble. They must know everything. Exactly. Or they'd never issue an offer like that. They'd never risk having a firm this small spit back in their face."

Now I was certain there would be more.

"So," Dwyer continued, "I think you better tell us everything about what you've been cooking up in Singapore with Bank of South Asia. What's the full story, my friend?"

I bristled at Dwyer's patronizing remark, tacked on to blandly assert his seniority over the room. I tried to curb my irritation, hastily absorb the extra rules in the game and the fresh positions of the players on the board.

"We have a deal with Bank of South Asia," I explained briskly, rushing to reach the words before they could be refuted. "Put together when I was in Singapore. We have contracts. Cash. An asset-backed line of credit for at least eighty million bucks secured by the Bangkok bonds. Then, last night when I call, I learn that BSA's suddenly fired their finance director, Stanley Man, who tells me BSA sold the financing contracts to Amsterdam Bank because Amsterdam was threatening to dump some large blocks of BSA stock from some of their insurance portfolios. And BSA buckled under because they live in constant fear of their reduced capital base with so much blood-letting in the Asian markets all last year."

Kyle pushed back in his chair impatiently. "Well. That's it, then."

"It would seem so," Ted Dwyer agreed.

Kyle added firmly, "That's the bitch of it."

I dashed after them to interrupt their momentum. My impatience swam like a carp beneath my skin bumping for escape. "We have contracts."

"What you have," Ted Dwyer declared, "is a legal fight that will take two years to get to court, take two million dollars to run, and take two more years to win." He paused to allow Kyle to mutter his accord. "In the meantime, what are you going to use to pay for those bonds?"

"Then," I insisted stubbornly, "let Bangkok Commercial sue us and let them wait a few years."

Kyle snorted. "And where would our next deals come from? Do you know of anybody that would put a deal through here if there's even a hint that we might not perform or that their deal might get sucked into some pending litigation that could jump out and bite us in the ass?"

"Only if there is any litigation. Bangkok Commercial will come to the same conclusion and not spend the time and money to chase us."

"Bankrupt for cash, Paris. Or bankrupt for reputation. It's all the same thing."

"But," I argued, "that's only if Bank of South Asia is really going to back out of the deal. We need to get to them directly. To their president and directors. Find out what the hell is really going on."

Kyle shrugged, cynical, broadcasting his scorn of such obvious simplicity. "You can if you like."

I could not understand why Kyle was conceding so fluently, and so haphazardly; his wrath would normally have been huge. Instead, his indifference was cast about the office in careless plenty.

Arrested as much by my own confusion as by Kyle's lofty dismissal, I ground my heels into the smooth carpeting under the scolding hum of the fluorescent lighting.

Kyle ploughed on. "Brenda, what's our current treasury position?"

Without hesitation she chimed it out with her customary efficiency. "We could sell off most of our short bonds and commercial paper, some of our equities. Raise twenty million. Draw another couple million on our credit lines if we had to."

"Dimitri, have we pre-sold any of those Bangkok Commercial bonds yet?"

In the thick Latvian accent that adhered to his English, Dimitri drawled, "Maybe ten million."

"What if you put on a fire sale this afternoon?"

"Maybe another ten million. Not more. We'd need about three or four more months after March tenth to sell off a full hundred million. That's why we could only do this with a massive credit line."

"Well, that about settles it." Kyle caught my eyes venomously.

It took all of my concentration to retain my balance and return his lethal stare.

In the stony quiet, with transparent ceremony, Kyle rose. "Please, all of you, listen very carefully. And, as of this minute, everything I'm about to tell you is absolutely confidential. The Securities Commission will prosecute you for insider trading if you act on any of it."

Kyle waited for our sketchy gestures of assent.

Kyle cleared his throat, bit back a burp on his morning coffee. "This was to be my year to retire. So we've been working on a merger to sell out to a major bank. To cash out the equity of all the founding shareholders and leave our remaining partners and staff with a clean start."

I was quickest to register, thirstiest for response. "Which bank?"

"That's why Ted's here," Kyle replied.

In unison, we swung our attention to the side of the room.

Dwyer settled back, masterfully drawing us in. Straightened his shoulders. "Atlantic Laurentide."

We waited for more details.

"At Kyle's request, I approached Atlantic a few months ago. Got them to agree on the numbers. And I've since been building a case for Senate approval and to smooth things over with the Securities Commission. We'd have everything cleaned up for late this year."

Listening to Dwyer explain it, I recognized, absolutely, like an approaching toll gate, the unfolding logic.

"Now that's going to have to change." Ted Dwyer ran his tongue around his gums as if burnishing his articulation. "I don't have to tell any of you that the Securities Commission will never allow this firm to be muscled into the brink of receivership by any foreign bank, including Amsterdam Bank."

"And," Kyle asserted, "I'm not about to walk out the door and be tarred for the rest of my life for one botched deal. Nor am I about to stand by and see this company come out on the short end of the stick from Amsterdam Bank to the tune of ten or twelve million bucks."

Ted Dwyer made an overt gesture of open palms with exaggerated shrug to indicate that there was nothing more to say. "So it's obvious. You clean up things before you pay for the bonds. Or you go on the block. And we sell you to Atlantic Laurentide."

"That gives us until March tenth, Paris. Three piss-poor weeks," Kyle repeated, shaking his head in grim admonishment.

The discord in Kyle's claim rekindled our recent grudges.

"You can't be so sure," I charged. "The Securities Commission. Stepping in to shut us down. We're not some huge multinational securities brokerage firm with offices all over the world. We're just a small investment bank with our fingers in a minor international deal."

"The banking and finance committee in the Senate sees it differently," Dwyer told me pointedly. "Sure, we're not London or

New York. I agree. As far as the international markets go, we're still some backwater farm team. Even Malaysia and Indonesia are better because, despite all their graft, they've at least got some action pumping away all the time. But what is it they always say in this country, Paris? Everybody in Canada hates Ontario. And everybody in Ontario hates Toronto. And everybody in Toronto hates Bay Street. And that's because, at least in this country, we've got the goddamn money. So this is the price we pay. We live in a fish bowl with the regulators watching our every move."

I made it obvious that I would not believe sight unseen.

Dwyer laid it out with prickly inflection. "The banking and finance committee is not about to ever let any bank or insurance company in this country fail and undermine public confidence in our finance industry. Biggest or smallest. Makes no difference to them. They are not about to let one ounce of public confidence, domestic or international, leak away."

Watching them as they waited for my response, I squinted suspiciously into midday sunlight that poured in abundantly from the wide windows behind Kyle. Watched their movements and expressions for evidence of disagreement. Waited for them to speak with any trace of indecision. Strove to dilute their authority.

Ted Dwyer pushed himself to his feet with a refined groan, hobbled over to the corner of Kyle's desk, his elderly eyes glassy and serene, and signalled an end to the discussion with an adept twist of his wrist to check his snug gold watch.

The meeting was concluded. I had lost their confidence. I had lost their respect. And I had lost their support. Inside myself, in a place where I could not deceive myself with my own indignation, I was forced to recognize that.

But I also knew, and had always known in that same place within myself, that I must reclaim the deal that had been stolen from me by BSA's forfeit to Amsterdam Bank. Regardless of my ambivalent posturing during the meeting, I knew I had no other choice. I must redeem myself, somehow, if not to salvage my career from indelible misfortune, then simply because I could not endure the least splinter of further loss. It was, I sensed, taking all I had to travel through each day to its tattered close. Morning to night, my stamina was melting like thin ice, unable to outlast even the weak winter sun.

"Well?" Kyle inquired.

"Well," I replied. I held in my objections, grinding down on them with my back teeth, waiting for Kyle and Ted to advance into the open, pronounce their penalty, expose their menace.

"Well, my friend," Dwyer declared, "looks like you're going to have to get us some straight answers out of Bangkok and Singapore."

"Because you think I can change their minds?"

"No," Ted Dwyer asserted dryly, "because the Securities Commission will be demanding them. And when they've got you in their sights for a couple of indictments for slipshod transactions that've bankrupted this firm, you better have something very convincing to say in your own defence or you could be looking at a couple of years in prison."

જી

Retreating behind my closed office door, I tried to heed the demands of my circumstances.

Like some stranger from outside the firm, I listened to the scraps of comments from colleagues as they passed by in the hallway. Their usually familiar voices seemed displaced, louder. Their babble swelled in my brain like a siren.

Two summers ago I had soared here, flying free of the rules, putting away two bond deals back-to-back without blinking in between. Some hundred million with Citibank and then twice that with Morgan Stanley. Seeming to live on nothing but the air between my words. Seeming to move at the speed of my own voice. On the phone all day wearing my throat hoarse across a handful of time zones; parked at my computer throughout the hollowed-out parts of the night. Four hours sleep a night. Calling in the money thirteen weeks straight in a single sprint. A bonus that became more bloated with each day's promises until it dwarfed a year's salary. Invincible as I outraced all of Kyle's doubt and criticism.

But now I sensed the gods had caught up with me, cornered me, my fears ever present like profanity whispered under my breath, failure snapping at my heels

I sensed I was moving through a time where every certainty had been undone.

I leaned into the embrace of its uncertainty and deceit.

∽∾

It was strange and misleading, the language of my profession.

Often we spoke in the expressions and vernacular of cowboys and gangsters; talking of gunning down our competitors, murdering them in the bidding, or ripping the guts out of the deal.

Yet none of these things was ever readily evident in the workings of the world we inhabited, where our physical contact with one another was all but eliminated. The true actions in our business days were conducted without wind-up and delivery; condensed into the electronic blips of telephone calls and facsimile transmissions; and freeze-dried into email. And the rules of engagement that governed our meetings and negotiations and transactions buried both our truths and our personal emotions many layers beneath our formal agendas and our dialogues. Webs spun with the silks of polite accord. The real drama was not in what was presented across the boardroom table, but in what was held back.

Our personal stars rose more on our prognostication for the money rather than on what we crafted with it. Ostensibly, our investments financed the construction of new factories, funded the research for break-through pharmaceuticals, or ensured the stability of pension plans for future generations. In reality, the money itself consumed our focus. We bet on endless tosses of a coin. At the altars within our firms, we were expected each morning to deliver newly minted foresight and planning, our reputations made and sustained by an alchemy of knowing in advance how investments would turn out, which choices to risk, which ones to avoid. Acclaim, and padded paycheques, showered down on us in the wake of our correct decisions like the sparkling tails of passing comets.

Closing a fat transaction, we sliced our success from a common loaf. Congregated afterwards in bars, celebrating with expensive Scotch that brought inebriation like a soft hand pushed into your face. And, knit together by our unguarded drunkenness, we collectively faced what we could not face alone: that the price of our privilege was paid in our indenture to careers that were fed by our own breath. We guessed out into the shadows. Trying to navigate by projections based on the shifting statistics of previous trading volumes and interest rate movements, the gap between what had occurred and what was to come often a mile wide, like using yesterday's tides to predict the high-water mark a year from now.

Moreover, our business dealings were much more a process of becoming rather than a process of being. Few deals were ever accomplished in crashing victories. For the most part, our deals and transactions were pieced together; journeys of a hundred miles, broken down into ten thousand steps. Revisions and alterations and repositioning swatted back and forth with our opponents as we pushed each other into default out of exhaustion; and everything gained inevitably required a further step to sustain it.

Nothing was ever really finished or complete.

You purchased an investment and then, each day, you had to decide anew whether to keep it or sell it. Constantly re-examining it. And the markets. And your cash resources. And your shifting investment objectives.

In making the decision to invest for a year, you forfeited a small piece of every day that followed for the daily determination necessary to maintaining the investment. Deal by deal, you mortgaged off slivers of your life.

I had watched those who did not understand this principle fail to practise any economy of decision. Men and women who were driven by their gluttony for triumph, scrambling to heft one transaction after another into the air; they pissed away their days a phone call at a time—stripping their lives to the bone, cannibalizing minutes from their personal lives, from family and friends—until it became impossible to continue juggling them all, and they were engulfed in the inevitable collapse.

And I had watched others; that compulsory burden of future decisions looming so large in their already overspent hours that they became paralyzed by it. I watched them become frozen in place; afraid to move forward; afraid to decide; no longer able to purchase and sell—money traders who lost their ability to trade the money. Inevitably, they deteriorated into some vanishing point on the horizon, as they were washed away by the restless waves of money surging forward around them.

I knew, no matter what else, I must protect myself from those outcomes by keeping my confusion tightly contained; I could feel the non-stop pressure of it within me, like a bag splitting against my ribs, and I had to keep pushing it down to prevent it from dilating into that same abandon or paralysis I had seen in others.

I sensed, now more than ever, I needed to keep myself poised, deftly treading a tightrope between the pull of my personal predicaments in two half-lived lives. Fighting my fears of racing to Singapore to salvage my career, and fighting my fears of remaining here to hang on to my lost life; at risk, both ways, of finding that what I pursued and what I clung to were equally barren.

Nothing ever really finished or complete.

8

Arriving home from the party, she goes directly to the bedroom, closing the door.

Our circle of friends, increasingly frayed by careers and stress and divorce, has been brought briefly back together by the first party of the summer, where we have been temporarily sustained around the barbecue by a surfeit of chilled Chardonnay and cold beer.

I stay out of the bedroom, checking locks and turning off lights, trying to avoid my awareness that I am deliberately lagging. So I stand in the darkened livingroom of our condo, watching, through the picture window, a summer storm finally burst through the June humidity, sheets of rain blowing down into the blue street lights. In the night outside, wet fingers of wind pull at the glass, drive the scattering drops across the washed curbs, out onto the slick streets and into the uneven flow of gleaming late-night vehicles.

When I go into the bedroom, she has already changed into a thigh-length cotton jersey with Toronto Blue Jays crest and her name stencilled across the shoulders—a gag gift for her thirty-fifth birthday from her law office last month.

She sits on the edge of the bed, not speaking.

I begin to undress.

"I've got to go to my office tomorrow," she reminds me. "We've got two commercial real estate deals closing back to back first thing Monday morning, so I've got to finish them up this weekend."

I nod.

I slide naked into the bed and roll onto my side with my back to her.

"Paris?"

Before I can answer, I have to shift my cheek up out of the pillow. "What?"

"Is there anything wrong between us?"

"No."

"I mean it, Paris. I need to know. You sure there's nothing wrong?"

I am slipping down a slope of tiredness. And I have drunk too much to open myself to her persistent doubt again. "No."

"It's just every time you get drinking at a party somewhere you're always talking about me being so dissatisfied that I'll be leaving you or divorcing you or something."

"I'm not."

"You are. You do."

"It's just all the medication you're on right now," I try to explain. "So you're not drinking. So everything moves at a different pace for you than it does for all of the rest of us who are drinking. We all make a million cracks like that and take a million shots at each other all night long."

"That's the best you can do?"

"Your depression. Your medication..."

"All me."

"No, Judith. We're both burned out. Really burned out. I'll tell you what, when you're at the office tomorrow, I'll see what I can do about getting a flight to Nassau or something. Get a week off.

Sometime this month. Before everyone else gets their kids out of school and all the summer travel starts. Just the two of us."

The silence is dense with her dissatisfaction.

I think about the rain outside, about how it drifts into footprints and eradicates the chronicle of your passing.

Finally, though, she switches off the light.

The darkness falls on me like a heavy blanket and I let my shoulders relax as it settles.

Still, I do not roll over to her.

While I want to tell her how much is going wrong between us, it is all I can do to try to sleep without dreaming.

9

Everything had become waiting now.

I was waiting for Kyle to return from his scheduled hour of straining with his trainer at his fitness club, when Michelle came again to my office.

Did I need to reassure her one more time? I wondered. Hold her hand until she got on the cruise ship?

"Mr. Smith?" She bobbed in the doorway of my office and blinked out from the ice-blue wheels of her glasses.

"Yes, Michelle."

"I just wanted to thank you for talking with me yesterday."

I shrugged, self-conscious without expecting to be. "My pleasure."

"I'm going to try that the next time someone on our street has a yard sale. Make my fortune in yard sales." She grinned at her joke.

"Okay." I realized she had helped me retrieve some misplaced part of my caring. I was grateful to her. Tried to give up an easy grin. "I'll help you corner the yard sale market."

"And." She inhaled excitedly. "I wanted to tell you that we're scheduled to dock in the Bahamas next week so I'm going to try to visit our new office there. In Freeport."

I was perplexed, delayed my desire to be alone to resume my

anxious preparation, searched my memory. "We have an office in the Bahamas?"

"Yeah. A brand-new one. Molly, Mr. Addison's secretary, just told me about it this morning."

"I didn't know."

"Well, I'm going to see them when we're there next week. And I'm going to tell them that they absolutely have to transfer me down there." She sighs lazily. "Wouldn't you just love to live in the Bahamas?"

"What would I do here without you?"

"Well, then I'll tell them that they don't get me unless they take you, too. We'll both transfer."

I laughed, allowing to myself that mirth over something so harmless was not fleeing my fatal struggle against Kyle and Bank of South Asia. "Okay. Deal."

She tripped away.

I was left puzzled. Wondering. Tiny beats of suspicion shooting up my chest.

ⁿⁿ

In Kyle's office, angling for Kyle's response, I cast my words into the expecting silence and then waited for the earliest ripples of reaction.

This was the practice of the telephone calls, of the meetings and of the negotiations that constituted my life. Knowing which words to emphasize, which to eclipse, which to avoid; what points to punctuate with pauses, what others to gloss over in dexterous delivery. How to read the pitch and pull in anyone's eyes or reply or silence. Reel in their agreement like taking a trout from a stream. My mastery of this practice, of getting to where I wanted, and then getting what I wanted, has driven the success of my dealings, and has compelled the gallop of my career, my life.

"Kyle, I can still bail this out. I'll head out to Singapore and Bangkok tonight."

"And do what?"

"We've still got some options there."

"Such as?" Rolling his shoulders, Kyle refused to be convinced, forced me to spell it out.

"Right now, this minute, I don't know exactly."

"My point," he huffed. "Exactly."

"Let me get there, find out who sold us out to Amsterdam Bank. Find…"

Yet now, the words began to break off faster than I could feel my mouth making them so that I could not be sure whether I had actually spoken them or whether they only floated up from my inner voices.

That I had said them, and that they had been heard, was only confirmed when I saw the disdain deepen in Kyle's face.

Instantly, I was rocked by an intense anger. As if I had been sucker-punched by Kyle's snub and sour pouting. I hungered to lash back in rebuttal. All of this, I realized sadly, had soaked up my patience, leaving me brittle. I tapered my tone, treading unfamiliar ground; I have had no practice in displaying weakness.

"Kyle," I explained arduously, "I just can't accept that this is final in Singapore."

"Why not?" Kyle splashed my attempt with his arrant doubt.

"Why do you think?"

"No. You tell me."

I struggled to recapture my advantage, trying to disarm Kyle with a display of compromise. "I know you and Ted Dwyer are right. But we're not being given all the facts. Just let me get to the bottom of this."

"I agree with Ted. I don't think we have any other choices, or chances, in this situation."

"You would." Kyle's willing dismissal of alternatives, and the oily undertones in his acceptance of our misfortune, was uncustomary; it did not persuade me.

"You may have got us into this. But Ted and I will get us out."

Refusing to respond to this, I tried to quit it. I felt as if I was moving backwards. Getting further and further away from the necessary truths.

"We all know," Kyle conceded in the silence I had left between us, "you've been under a strain since the unfortunate events in your life last summer."

"Unfortunate events?"

"You know what I mean, Paris."

I hated the way that it was painted. So diminished. "Unfortunate events?"

"Fine." Kyle dropped his open palms onto the desk. "Since your wife. Since then, we know you've been under a strain. We've been hoping that you'd take some time off. More than just three days. And you keep telling me that you'd rather keep working. That work is best for you. And you just keep getting more strained. And now this. Based on this, I think we better get you some professional help."

"Professional help?" I let the words rebound, replete with their implications.

"Fine, then. You go back to Singapore without our blessing. Without our mandate to legally represent us. And you just stir up a lot more confusion and damage so that this can never get cleaned up."

"And?"

"And we demand you get professional help. Even if you quit we put that permanently in your record. In every record. In every reference. In every reference check. Emotional instability. How far will you get when you try to obtain a new position somewhere else?"

"I could sue for discrimination. And wrongful dismissal."

I felt us stumble in unison as we both hesitated, both tempted to lunge at the bait; and then felt it as we both desisted, assessing too little profit in it.

Kyle steered around it, accelerated beyond it. "No doubt in anyone's opinion that you're the best we've got. Best I've seen in a long time. But you can't keep working just to drive yourself into the ground on your own personal agenda and leave the rest of us hanging out in the wind."

As much as I wanted to argue it out, something within me warned me that Kyle's censure and insinuation would continue to escalate. I knew I had been dancing myself into exhaustion for months, and lying to myself that it did not show to everyone around me. I knew Kyle could cite witnesses throughout the firm. I would never have enough stamina to refute them all. Instinctively, I hoarded my energy to see what waited around the bend.

"You're always so sure, Paris. That you have the right answer. You always move so fast around here. As if you don't ever need anyone else."

I tried to slip my response back to Kyle as a question rather than a statement to diminish the antagonism and contain the allegation. "And haven't I always delivered?"

"What if Bangkok Commercial hadn't come around to us when you re-submitted our bid? What about the bonds you had let us start selling at pre-subscription prices? Where the fuck would we have got them from? With no deal from Bangkok Commercial we would have had to buy them in the open market in order to meet our deliveries. Probably at a higher price than we sold them for. And buying high and selling at a loss is no fucking way to stay in business."

With effort, I remained acutely silent, stripping Kyle's declaration of any finality and forcing him to stumble into ill-prepared debate. He grumbled onward.

"The firm is exposed. We still have our ass hanging out through the seat of our pants. What if Bangkok Commercial Bank doesn't back out of the deal now that it's come unravelled in Singapore. And we're still supposed to come up with the ninety-two-million cash discount payment for a hundred million in bonds by March tenth. What are we supposed to do? Go to work for Amsterdam Bank for peanuts?"

"Why," I demanded, "are you so adamant that there's no solution? Why are you so convinced that there's no other option?"

"Maybe our only real option is Atlantic Laurentide."

"Oh. Yeah. And thanks for letting me know that you and Ted Dwyer were hatching up that little plot. Nothing like being kept in the dark inside your own firm. Christ! Now I don't even know that we're opening up an office in the Bahamas. What next, you going to put us out on the street with hotdog carts?"

"What Bahamas?"

"Bahamas. Apparently we've now got an operation in Bahamas."

"No. Not by any stretch. Not a chance."

"Then what's Molly talking about?"

"Obviously something that, as a secretary, she doesn't know shit about. And shouldn't be talking about. And something I'm going to have to talk to her about. Right fucking quick."

Kyle snorted vigorously.

His pause permitted me to consolidate my posture and my proposal. "Give me this much, Kyle. Let me get Singapore on the phone later tonight. Let me get to the chairman of BSA. Let me speak with Albert Quan. This thing can't be a dead issue. Not after all the work I put in on it. Not after all the contracts we signed. There's got to be some room left in it to move back and forth. Let me get hold of Albert Quan and shake him around."

"Okay, Paris. Fine. Do that. Get hold of the fucker. Shake him. Bounce him. Threaten him. Sell him your sister. I don't care. Just don't dig us into a hole any deeper than this already is."

Kyle came to a tremulous halt, as if colliding with the reverberation of his own overly strident words.

Yet I sensed something more, something inconsistent to the unbending belligerence of his glare; in the chancy twist of his heavy shoulders in his ill-fitting suit, I sensed some falseness leak from Kyle.

So I stood reticently in Kyle's broad stare, refraining from my urge to argue anything further in my defence, leaving nothing for him to accost or belittle, making clear my determination to prevail.

Cheated of final finger pointing, Kyle pasted his scepticism and discontent in his fidgety grimace.

✦✦✦

My twice-repeated attempt to reach Albert Quan was channelled in jerks through the switchboards and secretaries at the Bank of South Asia. After a short final wait on hold, the receiver filled with Albert Quan's smoothly brushed articulation.

"Good morning Mr. Smith. Or should I say good evening. How nice to hear from you."

(I'll bet.)

"Mr. Quan, I'm calling you directly because we still have some critical business to complete. And Stanley Man has just told me he's no longer with your bank."

"We were sorry to accept Stanley's resignation."

(Yeah.)

"I spoke with Stanley yesterday. There's some misunderstanding about the credit line we arranged with you. For the Bangkok Commercial Bank bond deal."

"I'm sorry. Our board could not approve that credit for you."

The words quivered within their own faint electronic echo, as if the line were a tunnel. They did not so much rankle as sap my confidence and leave me vulnerable. My fears and concerns shoved rudely from behind like someone impatient in line in back of me. Jostled toward the centre of my frustrations, I tapped out my tension with my fingernails against the plastic shell of the receiver, little flashes of noise at the rim of my ear.

"Mr. Quan, you're wrong. Your board did approve that credit line. Your board gave us that credit line. For eighty million."

"No. That was never approved."

(Bullshit!)

"Mr. Quan. We have your letter of intent. Your contracts and undertakings. All signed. You signed them. Sealed them. We have faxed copies."

"I regret to report that I never signed. I did not sign."

"We have your signature."

"Then it's been forged."

"And our fax copies show that all documents were executed under bank seal."

"Then you have also been deceived about that."

"No."

"Mr. Smith. There is no credit line to your bank. Because all credit facilities greater than ten million dollars must be approved by our full board of directors. Your credit line was not. You will find no reference to your credit line in any board meeting minutes. And no resolution passed by our board to grant the credit facility. And that is the only process that legally commits this bank to any lending."

"But we have contracts. Signed and sealed."

"If you have such documents, Mr. Smith, then you have some confidential information about why we accepted Stanley Man's resignation."

"What do you mean?"

"We discovered numerous discrepancies in Mr. Man's files. We requested his resignation for malfeasance with regard to your file. And other files."

"Your signature?"

"Obviously a forgery."

"And your corporate seal?"

"Also illegal. And not binding."

"I don't believe you."

"I'm afraid it's not about what you believe. It's what is legal for this bank and what is not legal and not binding for this bank."

"And where does Amsterdam Bank come into all of this?"

"I was not aware that your application included any mention of Amsterdam Bank."

"No. What is your bank doing with Amsterdam Bank?"

"I don't have that file in front of me, so I'm not familiar with all of the details."

"Some of them?"

"My understanding is that Stanley had incurred some very large expenses from two law firms for diligence and for legal opinions on the bond prospectus that was submitted as collateral for the asset-backed credit line. In the range of a quarter-million dollars in legal fees if I'm not mistaken. When we began to uncover all of the discrepancies in Stanley Man's files, we had an opportunity to discuss your particular transaction with representatives of Amsterdam Bank. They agreed to compensate us for our high legal costs for the diligence and opinions on the bond offering, so we were happy to turn our file over to them. Essentially, we sold our diligence and legal work to them."

"I don't believe that."

"I'm sorry."

(Fuck me, you're sorry.)

"What about Amsterdam Bank threatening to dump your stock and drive down the value of your equity?"

"I'm afraid I don't understand."

"Tell the truth."

"Mr. Smith, I've just told you the whole truth."

"And I'm not satisfied with it. We're not satisfied with it."

"Well, Mr. Smith. I've done all I can. When matters such as these remain at an impasse, I'm bound by our bylaws to turn them over to our solicitors. I can request that they send you a letter if you prefer."

"What I would prefer is the credit line, the money. As agreed. As promised. As per signed contracts!"

"I can only repeat this one last time."

"Repeat what?"

"There is no contract. There is no credit. There is no money!"

The call was cut off with a clunking sound, and I was left with the drone of a dead line.

Stupidly, I sat there and continued to hold the receiver to my ear, listening intently to the steady tone, hoping for some reason to hear more words or breathing or even footsteps walking away.

When there was nothing, I replaced the receiver in the cradle cautiously, tentatively, my hand poised to scoop it back up at the first sound of life.

I drew a thick breath and blew it out forcefully through my pursed lips. I knew I was confused, even frightened; and angered, immensely angered, that someone had done this to me. I licked my lips, tasting salty sweat that I had not expected, tried to concentrate beyond the drumming of the artificial breeze that came down into my office from the vents and ducts of the heating system.

I could feel the fragile equilibrium and brief momentum that I had so recently induced in these hours now begin to give way, leaving me like some vital fluid seeping from a fatal wound.

I tried to listen for some voice to guide my next immediate actions by sitting as still as possible; but nothing would come.

What must I wait for?

のひ

More than an hour after my call with Albert Quan, I found myself still at my desk, alone in the office, without being able to adequately retrace my journey to the end of the day, my activity now stalled while I waited out the clock on my side of the world. Night in Toronto, with closed doors, people gone home and my options crippled by Albert Quan's denial; while, in Singapore, the morning brightened and the day broadened, allowing Albert Quan to deal and manoeuvre, further increasing his perjury and his advantage.

Tired, I sat there, holding myself still, my neck rubbery with exhaustion, trying to determine my next move.

Leave now? Return home? To what?

At home, no sleep again last night. Or, at least, no easy sleep.

Finally closing my eyes for a few hours on the living room couch, now a familiar retreat, I sank beneath the surface only to have my sleep crumble away near dawn, bringing me into a false grey light, hemmed in by my own doubt.

At their centre, my nights dried up, cracked open. Letting

ghosts into the unused spaces between thinking and dreaming. The ghosts that slipped through the cracks were not the ghosts of people, but the ghosts of places. Of times.

I came from my restless dreams suddenly and severely, never certain of when I had been sleeping or when I had ceased. I was just, abruptly, awake at a hollow cavity in the darkness. Immediately, I was overwhelmed with vivid recollections of times when I had travelled with her, of places we had been together, of experiences we had shared. Re-breathing extinct minutes of times when I had not been enveloped in the loneliness that was her absence.

It was as if I were watching photographs of towns and cities we had driven through. Streets we had pitched along and buildings we had approached and passed. A restaurant with an archaic hand-printed breakfast-special card sagging in the window, faded yellow and illegible from the afternoon glare. Storefronts boasting blow-out sales. Parks with rusted basketball hoops. Busy self-serve gas bars. Coca-Cola signs. It kept coming back to me: the two weeks we had driven through rural New England on our honeymoon.

None of the scenes ever ran long enough for me to fully identify them, always dissolving to a new scene before I could recall the plot. A disjointed movie pasted together from scraps on the cutting room floor. Scenes of non-specific locales: of traffic-light intersections and stop signs at street corners with bluntly pruned shrubs. Where I would remember myself yearning for my new wife at my side, yearning for the day's driving to be over so that I could hold her. Our love for each other carried along with us from place to place like our clean clothes.

We were for the first time strangely insulated from the persistent pace of our separate lives; and for the first time exempted from having to compromise our personal lives to our professional lives. It was so totally opposite from the evenings and weekends during the months previous to our marriage, where we were thrown together at the peripheries of our working days, making do with leftover minutes after we had allowed ourselves to be bled of all energy by our contrary careers.

In our car, I was left with nowhere to go except to slide deeper into my desire to sustain her.

My deepest emotions, still unfaded and undispersed in my memories, were my love for her mixed with my fear that I would fail her and her illness would overtake us both.

During the indulgence of those two weeks away from my office, I began wondering about the lives of the people passing by us on those streets and sidewalks, speculating about their joys and disappointments, always searching for the secret struggle of aspiration and hope in some isolated face that would give me insight into making our own happiness endure; and, as I drove away, always away, leaving them behind as we moved on, the insight always eluded me like some sought-after name or song dancing beyond the tip of my tongue. My remembered passage somehow now becoming a measure of things unsaid, of time lost, and of love expended.

Nor could I stop these scenes, these pictures, from coiling up through my thoughts in the vacant darkness of my sleepless nights, no matter how I re-bunched my pillow and sought to return to my fitful sleep of anxious dreams. The places and days and persons now seemed my mortgage for the happiness I had owned with her. Not so much agitating in themselves as in my inability to control them when I could not prevent them from returning of their own accord in the empty hours. They confused me. And wrenched me. As much as I loved going back to her, I could no longer stand the fresh pain of losing her again each time I plunged back into the present.

Could I admit it? When the scenes would not cease, when I could not escape them and their cadence of days spent, now irretrievable, they brought blinking tears.

Perhaps more unsettling was that these memories of unknown faces, then and now, were verities of other lives everywhere. Everywhere existing. Everywhere enjoying and suffering. All averring that I was not singular and unique, regardless of my distress and dilemma, and not exempted from the usual course of cause and effect in life, nor released from the promises I had made to my company to succeed, and to myself to let her go.

Sitting there at my desk, I spread the wings of my shoulder blades and arched my neck until I could feel the grinding in my upper vertebrae, trying to shed some of the collected fatigue. I could not recall ever being so empty and aching.

Would the tide of my pain, I wondered, ever begin to recede? The moon that had pulled it seemed now flung too distant to reach back to me.

Did I even really know who I was any more? Now that she was gone.

Had I, since it had happened seven months ago, begun to dis-cover that I was a previous person trapped in a new life? Our silvery spider plants, after she moved them in from the balcony at the end of the summer and transplanted them into smaller pots, had died because their roots were too large, too mature, too spread from their previous life. Would the same happen to me now that I was transplanted into a life made smaller without her?

Had I ever really known who I was?

Invariably, my career was always my definition of myself. I was a thirty-eight-year-old investment banker, ten years ahead of my age in my career. Then I was married, her husband; and then I was a vice-president. Because I had been in my career longer than I had been in my marriage or in my office, the former had, like water running longer over rock, worn deeper grooves into me.

I forced my neck back again, trapping a breath, releasing it reluctantly.

I retreated into my work to avoid stretching my awareness that I was trying to out-race my fear; squeezing my eyelids and my shoulders with equal vigour in an attempt to burst through to some solution.

I brought my weight forward in the chair, reached to the telephone, pulled the receiver to my ear, and nicked the long sequence of buttons to bring Stanley Man's voice back to me from the heat and humidity on the other side of the world.

"Got through to Albert Quan, Stanley."

"Good or bad?"

"Bad, Stanley. Worse than you laid out. Not just you getting axed. But our financing has been yanked out from under us. We're dead in the water at BSA."

"So what's your next move?"

"If I can't get the money to pay for the bonds, then I better do something about the bonds."

"You going to see Bangkok Commercial Bank?"

"You see any better way around it?"

"Afraid not."

"Can you meet me in Bangkok the next couple of days?"

"Not like I'll be missed at the office."

"I need you to bring all of the contracts, all of the files, everything you've got on your computer. I'll email my itinerary."

"I'll be waiting."

I lifted myself from my chair, turning to face out into the winter darkness.

Breathing out of balance.

I recognized, instinctively, by nature and training and habit, that I rose too readily to the least adversity; always forcing myself to finish my work, even when my eyes burned with fatigue, to finish my treadmill exercise even when my shins throbbed. But that had nothing to do with why I could not walk away from this, writing it off to the callous deceit of Albert Quan, soaking up the financial losses by negotiating with Amsterdam Bank. To accept my failing in this enterprise would bring a consequence larger than I could absorb in my life. I would never be able to escape it, the echoing of guilt and avarice, because it would become fused with her memory, which would always be with me. To bring this deal back from Bangkok last summer, I had left her alone.

In wanting more than too much, I had ended up with less than too little.

Maybe nothing.

Those realizations, adhering one to another, wove themselves into a greater fabric of fault and blame. I tried focusing away from them, looking out, out into the inky expanse of cold and remote stars, only to be met by the huge indifference of the night sky.

I had nothing. Nothing that could be taken up until I left this side of the world. No idea of what would happen to me until I arrived on the other side of the world. No escape from myself either place. And, in between, no idea of when she would release me. Or how.

Suspended.

Life on hold.

∽∾

I edged up the hallway on the balls of my feet, certain I was alone yet somehow fearful of disturbing the resonant vibrations of the empty offices.

Through Kyle's doorway.

Over to Kyle's desk.

Looking for something. What?

Something to confirm that Kyle was concealing some lie. Some evidence that would allow me to depart with the minimum comfort of verifying that, if I did not know everything, at least I could determine that I was being deceived.

This was the harsh legacy of my telephone call with Albert Quan.

The voice comes. Insistent. I could not deny that, if I had not known there were manipulative and self-serving men in Singapore and Bangkok, I should have known. That they had deceived me was not solely their design; it was as much my fault because I deliberately refused to invest in doubt or furnish even peripheral suspicion or mistrust. I had intentionally discarded my caution to certify to myself that, within this massive bond transaction constructed of my own hand, caution was redundant because the enterprise was supported by my foresight and abilities.

It was not about my ascending an ordained arc of success. It was about how I had survived my journey through the last seven months.

I had to face it now. Through the last seven months I had needed this bond transaction to progress without the least delay or disruption, not only because I had been sustaining myself through my work, but also because the successful completion of this particular transaction would justify my leaving Toronto to travel to Bangkok last July.

So there must now be something more.

In the unnerving silence, courted by my misgivings, I let my gaze roam the unguarded papers and files littering Kyle's desk top. Carefully, I lifted several pages at random. Opened the two desk drawers cautiously.

Nothing.

I went back out to Molly's work station. Performed a similar audit of the files and paperwork stacked on her desk. When that also yielded nothing, I brought her dormant computer screen to life by brushing my fingers against the mouse. Snaked my way into her computer files. Tapped out the keyboard commands to search her files on the word "bahamas." The drive hummed compliantly. The screen flickered, posting a single result: "Global Vest Banking Corporation (Bahamas) Ltd." Instantly, I clicked on the file to open it. Only to be met with a stubborn demand for a password.

Fuck!

I tried several obvious ones based on permutations of Molly's name, Kyle's name, the firm's name. All invalid.

I was left standing there, staring down at the screen, the computer clucking obstinately against my finger flicking at the mouse or keys.

Frustrated.

Waiting... for what?

10

oming and going.

I sit in the airport lounge with my wife, the reckless momentum of our lives temporarily arrested by our commitment to take a vacation and by airline schedules that we cannot coerce with our appointment books the way we do our other hours.

An endless river of noise arising from the unremitting movement of people flows over us, and leaves us like two pieces of flotsam trapped together in our own swirling eddy; magnifying, in this vast public place, our intimacy beyond anything that it has been in remembered months.

A similar thing, I now recall, had happened when I had brought my father to the airport earlier in the year to return him, at the conclusion of his widower visit, compressed into a pair of clumsy weeks, to Florida. On that occasion, we had conveniently let a dubious silence settle upon us like a fresh skin to mask any hint that each suspected the other of contemplating a return to loneliness in his home.

"Do you want some coffee?" I ask her.

We have left the house at five in the morning, driving into a tattered June sunrise, squeezed down onto the highway under a blanket of smog and dewy grey humidity to make this seven o'clock flight. Now, Caribbean sunshine and fresh sea breezes await us, only a few hours off.

She shakes her head, blinking her sleep-deprived and red-rimmed eyes with obvious discomfort in the harsh airport brightness.

"I'm really looking forward to this holiday," I tell her.

"I can't believe we're going to Nassau in summer," she says. "When it's already hot here."

"Best I could do. Everything close to home will be mobbed with mom and dad and the kids out of school. And this is the only time I can get off. I've got to head out to Bangkok the day after we get back."

She is silent; deliberately, I recognize, unresponsive.

"It's important," I explain. "I'm on to something really big for the end of the year."

"You never can, can you?"

"What?"

"Stop." Her word coming back dry and brittle.

Beyond that, I know she is no longer able to advance.

"I'm going to grab a coffee. Sure you don't want anything?" I ask.

"Nothing."

As I start to return, sipping bitter black coffee through a peeled-back hole in the plastic lid, I peer across the cup at my waiting wife, studying her tired face from an angle outside of her periphery she will not detect.

I begin to think about stretching out with her on cool sheets, safe within the refuge of the tropic heat. Not fucking. But afterwards. With her rested and not so sharply worn. Connected and in love with each other. Touching. Whispering.

The emotional imprint of that vision remains so strong within me that, as I slide down in the fibreglass seat next to her, I ask, "What are you looking forward to most?"

"Just doing nothing," she sighs. "Just being left alone to do nothing. I'm so fed up with so much of the crap that's gone on all year, I just want to be left alone. My office just keeps piling on the real estate files when they know I really want litigation work. My psychiatrist nagging at me all the time to keep taking all that damn medication." Her syllables begin to race, whipped about within her dry mouth by anti-depression medication churning through her bloodstream. "And you're no help. Never home. I mean, what the hell is that all about? Let everybody and everything go to hell all week for all I care. I just don't want anybody or anything near me. I just want to be left alone."

My disappointment swells up into my face on the fragile tendril of coffee steam.

Do I, I ask myself, have any right to expect that she will have desires similar to my own? Should I even expect anything any more?

"See if we're boarding on time, will you?" she asks. "I can never hear those damn announcements in all this racket. Go up and ask at the desk."

Unexpectedly eager to be alone, I go up.

11

At thirty-five thousand feet over the black bowl of the Pacific Ocean I came up from sleep as if tripped by a wire at my ankles.

The fingertips riding on my shoulder are somehow erroneous; and ineffectual. I have mislaid my capacity to be comforted by someone's touch.

My eyelids fluttered open. Midway through the flight; midway through the night. The business-class cabin lights have been dimmed. As I focused my sleep-blurred vision, the delicate scent of Rive Gauche wafted up into my face. Judith came to me. Our life, before she became submersed in the riptide of depression. To the office she always wore the subdued spices of Chanel No. 19 sprayed at her wrists. But, on weekend evenings, when we would fervently escape—to drinks, dinner, music—the weekdays that had distanced us in separate careers, she wore the floral bouquet of Rive Gauche on her neck. And on the inside of her thighs. The fragrance seducing me as much as her body heat when she leaned against me in the elevator at the end of the evening, her face flush with lust let loose by the wine.

As I sat in the half-empty business-class section of the plane, the sudden impact of Judith's perfume in my nostrils produced a slew of such memories that filled me with fragile pleasure, then fled upon my next breath despite my attempt to hold them tightly within me at some juncture of dream and desire. I longed for them to be something I could wrap within my fist.

The woman had removed her fingers from my shoulder.

With her hand back on her own armrest she leaned across the aisle. "Are you all right?"

I laboured to smooth out my thoughts, and to soothe my tongue where I had bitten it in my sleep, reaching for my answer.

I swallowed dryly, relieved to let my final contact with the remaining dream fragments boil off. "I'm fine."

"I'm sorry I woke you," she said.

I did not immediately know how to respond, was not immediately sure I wanted to surrender the last traces of her perfume.

"You were mumbling, crying, in your sleep," she explained. "You woke me. I thought you would be embarrassed if you woke some of the others."

I struggled to remember my dreams. Normally restricting myself to drinking water on these prolonged flights in order to increase my effectiveness for business meetings imminent upon landing, I had this time tried to use a string of Scotches to suppress my fatigue and anxiety. The alcohol had, instead, induced an interval where I was too tired to keep my eyes open, but too restless to sleep. I had hovered behind my closed eyelids. The voice had caught up with me in those shadows, hissing into my unguarded thoughts reminders of my own mortality. It had coerced me to question whether my consciousness would remain stuck to my soul like some bubble gum when I died, so I would be aware of my own death, breathing out the last of my gravity as I lost my anchorage in this world. From that dubious perch, I had tumbled into harsh dreams.

"Thank you." I was grateful. But I also worried. In my impatience to reverse the collapse of my career over the failed bonds, I felt like I wanted to move invisibly through life right now, as if I would be slowed, or burdened, by the weight of anyone's attention; as if my disguise of sureness and confidence would not bear up under the least scrutiny of another human being.

"You're really perspiring. Are you running any flu or fever?"

Touching my face with my fingertips, I was surprised to find my chin and cheeks slippery with sweat. I swiped at them with the back of my band.

"Here," she told me. She dug into a lumpy handbag on the seat beside her, produced a packaged towelette.

I took it from her with a nod of appreciation, ripped it open and ran the lemon scented paper napkin over my face, behind my neck, the alcohol in the solution stinging at first contact to the pores on my chin, then bringing cooler relief as it evaporated.

"Better?"

"Yes," I agreed, "thank you."

"Try to replenish some of your fluids. If you start with orange juice rather than water, it'll also bring your glucose and your electrolytes back up. Then, if you keep perspiring, you can always take some aspirin to bring down any low-grade fever to make you a little more comfortable until we land."

I was confused by how quickly my need for distance was supplanted by my desire to have someone care about me, as if one overflowed the inadequacy of the other. Unbalanced more by this awareness than any appreciation of her, I tried harder than I should to deliver a friendly response. "I was going say something about the old joke to take two aspirins and call me in the morning. But you sound like a doctor. Are you?"

I coasted to a pause, waiting on her reply.

"Well," she revealed carefully, "I'm a doctor. But let's hope you don't have to call me in the morning. Or ever."

"Why not?"

"Because I'm a haematologist. And, with where I concentrate my practice, if they have to call me in for a consult, chances are you're terminal."

"Then we'll not hope for that."

She smiled faintly, politely. "No."

With her remark bringing our exchange to an obvious conclusion, I extracted myself by announcing, "I'll go down to the galley and get them to find some orange juice."

If she nodded or made any other non-verbal response, I did not wait to notice. I felt I owed it to her to leave my seat quickly and quietly in order to let her know that I would not take advantage of her compassion, and to allow her to rearrange herself back within the minimal privacy afforded by her seat and armrest.

By the time I returned, she had switched on her reading lamp, and was leaning forward in the sole cone of light within the dim cabin of dozing passengers, reading pages in a file taken from a briefcase open on the vacant seat next to her. She read intently, through wire-rimmed glasses, chewing absent-mindedly on her ballpoint pen.

I resumed my seat, sipping at the orange juice.

Jostled on city streets, crowded in elevators, pushed through the airport rituals of check-in and security, shuffling to board the flight, I was conscious of how I had been trying to hold myself away from being touched by anyone, clenching in my elbows when standing in lines, squeezing in my knees when seated in the waiting areas; not so much protecting myself as conserving myself for the impending intrusion of meetings and negotiations that would require me to remain engaged without limit or relief.

The money imposed harsh deadlines and harsher penalties. You didn't file contracts before their dates expired; you didn't conclude a deal before your purchase option expired; you didn't sell the stock before your financing defaulted back to the lender: you failed. No second chances. No get-out-of-jail-free cards. It didn't matter if you had already worked a week with minimal sleep; it didn't matter if you had a migraine for two days; it didn't matter if your wife was sick.

Past experiences of prior business negotiations accompanied me. In my mind, I leapt ahead into agitated encounters with directors at Bank of South Asia where I would have to negotiate upwards from a position of weakness through relentless will-power. Enduring yards of argument for every inch of progress. Outlasting them by forfeiting control over my own schedule and circumstance, always available when they were, always prepared before they were. Winning their trust with my constancy, attending meetings without excuse or delay, preparing without rest or relief. And throughout, my intelligence agile, eluding every snare of frustration and resentment; and artful, bringing them to appreciate my compromises

I searched for some way to shelter my meagre energy from my racing thoughts.

The aisle between our seats provided a comforting moat.

Slipping my lowered voice beneath the other resting passengers, I asked her, "Did I sleep through any changes in schedule?"

She looked up from her pages, wrinkled her nose to shift her glasses slightly. "I can never remember to keep moving my watch forward. I only know that it's been about eighteen hours since we left so we land in Singapore in about four or five hours."

"Business?" I inquired, nodding at the file on her lap.

"Pardon?"

I recognized that she had not awarded me enough attention to catch my quick inference, realized I might be intruding; yet was sufficiently driven by my nervous anticipation of impending meetings, and by my desire of safe contact with someone I could trust because they were a stranger, that I explained. "The paperwork. You're obviously travelling on business."

"AIDS," she explained.

"You're in research?"

"Research and treatment," she conceded. "Haematology."

"Both in Singapore?" I inquired, cautioning myself that, if she did not respond further, I better quit before I was perceived as pestering her.

"Meetings with a research team in Singapore that I've been involved with for the last few years. Then to Bangkok to present my paper at the World Health Organization AIDS conference."

When she did not reciprocate by inquiring about my profession, I was reminded that it should end there according to business travel etiquette.

Yet she was the first person, the only person, from outside my office, from outside my industry, that I had come even remotely close to in over two hundred days of grinding out hours at the office and burning up hours at home. In my work, I had used my isolation to conceal my loss and loneliness, always fearful that, if I shared them, they would betray me. Knowing that she could not divulge my watered-down and eroded emotional state to Kyle or my colleagues undermined my resolve, allowing the heartache I had been so severely suppressing to rise; like trying to hold back water with my bare fingers. My hungering to break through to her was so sudden and so overwhelming that I could not sense if it was need or desire, or both, and it caused me to betray my privately predicated boundaries, even caused me to betray Judith by leaving her behind for a moment.

I held my tone distinctly level and did not let it creep up into the register of a re-started conversation. "Can I ask you a question?"

She shrugged. "I suppose so."

"Do you see a lot of people die in your work?"

Instantly, I watched her eyes trace me as she judged my authenticity, my legitimacy. (Who are you?) Her sanction was registered in a slight quick shake of her head, her short dark hair curling at her neck and shoulders. "More than I'd like."

"Does anyone ever ask you why people die?"

"They usually ask, 'Why me?' or 'What did I do to deserve this?'...I'm the one who's always simply asking why."

"Do you have any answers?"

"The only answer I ever seem to have for myself," she admitted, "is that I know more and more about how people die. But I never know why."

Somehow I knew to wait for more.

"Usually," she continued, "the only people who ask about dying are people with some incidence currently impacting their life."

In the silence that she left hanging between us in the aisle, I recognized that, like lifting a leaf at the tip of a branch, she had exposed a small part of herself.

Wanting to reciprocate, I admitted clumsily, "I lost someone recently."

In the completion of my statement I discovered that I had plotted no course beyond the general reckoning of my question.

"I'm Paris Smith," I added.

"Wilma Russo."

In return, I refrained from offering my hand, hoping to make it clear that it was not an impersonal business introduction.

"Your loss in your bad dreams?" she asked courteously.

I stalled. I was afraid to let on the abandonment I knew, the confusion and listless lack of direction I felt. "I don't know."

She hesitated, transparent in holding back some additional inquiry, perhaps taking my minimal response as a cue not to pry further.

Although unease of any focus on my own concerns flickered, my next words seemed to rise up out of me like a balloon breaking its tether. "Does everyone with AIDS die?"

Barely, almost imperceptibly, she allowed herself a subtle sigh. "The tertiary cases that I see do. By the time I see them, they've all reached full-blown AIDS. And they all eventually die."

I was unexpectedly relieved to sense her sad acknowledgment of her terminal patients. I had spent the last months imagining myself on some one-way street, racing to leave the locations of my past life behind, pouring my haste and exertion into my career, at the loss of my competence to reach outward. Instead of serving up some shallow consolation, I tried to offer her an opportunity to speak further and risked telling her, "So you keep pushing yourself longer and harder. Trying to help them all before the clock runs out."

In her eyes, in a single tired blink, she admitted it, but refused to voice it; only replied banally, "And now you're my doctor?"

I shrugged self-consciously. "Sorry."

I wished to wrap the conversation into a graceful loop, but I began to feel as if I was losing my way. I tried to make myself think it was because, married, it had been some years since I had been in this situation of speaking closely and personally with another woman; not discussing business in meetings; not idle inquiries with secretaries and waitresses. Yet I could not fully deceive myself with the blanket amnesty offered by matrimony, and had to face a thorny truth. I employed my isolation. I used it to keep the door closed on my remorse for not sustaining Judith with more energy as I grew increasingly frightened of failing her and losing her. In the perpetual pace of my work, I had constructed an environment that had forbid pausing to speak of it with myself, with anyone. That doubt and loneliness overtook me now that I was forced to a halt, immobile within the confines of the aircraft cabin, suspended not so much over the ocean as from thrusting myself forward into the urgent negotiations I sought with Albert Quan.

As I faltered, her face tightened in her concentration on me and I clearly received the broadcast of her thoughts. (Are you for real or are you playing to me?)

Were all of my progressions now to be misdirected?

I was anxious that these few moments of being able to trust someone not be absorbed back into the other interruptions and postponements at the core of my life. I needed the reassurance of having one small thing go from start to finish without diversion or delay.

Slipping by the impending rejection of her tapered response, I plummeted recklessly to the end of our conversation. "Would you like to get together in Singapore? Talk some more over dinner? A drink after work?"

"Thank you, but no. I'll be very busy. My schedule is really crammed up. Thanks anyway." She was firm and fast and fixed.

It did not surprise me that she was so well practised in fending off overtures; she was attractive, but I had trusted her not to read more into my invitation than what it had been, so I believed her without question. I nodded again in appreciation of her attention; leaned back into the shadows of my seat, courteously allowing her to return to her work without further interruption.

Toronto to Vancouver.

Vancouver to Singapore.

On a map it was a couple of easy hand spreads.

Out of my life it was an intermission of twenty-six hours, cancelled off the clock as soon as the ticket was handed across the check-in counter.

Suspended in the air. Suspended in time. You could try to read or work or cast off the hours with in-flight movies, but you could only side-step the fact that your life was on hold—from the events you left behind on departure and the events that awaited you on arrival.

I closed my eyes, to locate some corner of my thoughts where my instincts resided sure and safe. My ears filled with the muffled drone of the engines and with the slipstream rushing along the skin of the aircraft. I was unable to tell whether I was moving forward in time and space, or whether it was moving in the opposite direction against me, leaving me behind as it passed.

12

On the Sunday we return from Nassau I go to the office without unpacking.

During our days on the beach, I limit myself to a brief review of email after morning coffee, determined to prevent my work from intruding into our lazy afternoons on the sand. But, throughout the return flight, surrounded by sunburnt couples sharing last drinks, Judith napping beside me, I become increasingly anxious. I am scheduled to fly to Southeast Asia the next morning for final negotiation of the bond proposal with the directors of Bangkok Commercial Bank. Shirking my preparation for those meetings to drink rum and woo my wife summons misgivings not felt since facing a college examination without studying.

I duck out the door mid-afternoon on a hasty apology, my worry about the coming week's meetings prevailing over my guilt of dodging the dark disappointment in Judith's face.

In the office, I rush against the clock, all the time struggling to force myself to return from the unhurried pace of days dribbled away under palm trees to the frantic dictates of the money. Hours dissolve as I read bundles of arid clauses that have landed on my desk from our attorneys in my absence, having to weigh the worth of each word. The revised clauses require me to re-calibrate bond payment schedules on my computer, sucking in fat columns of

numbers to stack and re-stack them like bricks in a wall; study-
ing Moody's and Standard & Poor's bond-yield curves that snake,
green and yellow and blue, back and forth across my computer
screen like the waves of a well-regulated heartbeat; prodding
myself to keep track of which documents are indispensable to my
negotiations as I stuff files into my briefcase for the trip.

Before midnight, I slide through the front door, some part of
me hoping Judith is asleep. She is not. We get trapped together in
the kitchen: she, angry that I am so late without calling; I, angry
that her illness no longer allows her to understand. Tense, futile
words.

She becomes tight-lipped. It is, I recognize, her holding herself
together against the frustration and anxiety that splash up over
the limits of her medication now that we are leaving our vacation
behind and resuming the full pace of our lives. She turns away
from me, standing in her housecoat and slippers at the stove, re-
heating soup while a frozen bagel, sliced in half, toasts under the
broiler in the oven.

After working an additional day within the one that has started
at a tropical sunrise, spending it shackled to my computer screen
with nothing passing my lips but endless rounds of coffee, I am
washed out, acutely hungry, impatient to eat, and irritated by
the wait. "I've got to leave for the airport in about five hours for
an early-morning flight. I need to grab some sleep."

"Just wait. This is a cream soup, it takes time or it scalds. If
you've waited this long, it's not going to kill you to wait a little
longer."

Petty malice has crept into her voice. It tempts me to declare
that I am flying halfway across the world on four hours sleep
because I have held our vacation intact despite late changes to
my business schedule. Instinctively, I know she cannot help her-
self, know I will regret it.

Ignoring her, I bend to the oven to observe my toasting bagel.

"Just leave that for a minute," she warns. "We cleaned the fridge out before we left for Nassau. I took it out of the freezer, it was frozen, I could barely cut it. It'll take a couple of more minutes."

"But it's toasted on the top already."

"It'll still be ice in the middle."

"But the top is going to burn."

"You can scrape off a little bit. If you'd called, I could have thawed it."

Bending further, I slip my hand around the edge of the partially open oven door.

"Just leave it."

"I'm just checking it."

I carefully balance my hand an inch above the hot pan and two inches below the glowing broiler element, stretching my fingers towards the foremost half of bagel.

"Just wait."

"I'm taking it before it burns."

Agitated by my movements and interference, leaning closer to the saucepan that she is stirring, her knee bumps into the oven door, popping it upward.

The closing door knocks my arm, and my hand jumps up against the cherry-red element. Catching by one knuckle, which sticks for a second. Sizzling. Sour-smelling steam issuing from the frying skin.

I jerk it free, and out of the oven.

"Goddammit!"

And I only need to look at her to see, and fully feel, her alarm and grief and sudden regret.

"Well it's your own damn fault," she bickers weakly. "If you just wait... only takes... I told you to wait... What do you expect coming home so late?"

At such times she has no defence against the least ounce of guilt from actions or accidents.

Slowly, her words running out, she places the soup spoon on the counter and pads off to the bedroom. Leaving me kneeling on the kitchen floor, sucking wetly at my stinging knuckle. Leaving me with what has now become a familiar distress of watching events so easily overpower her failing abilities to cope with them. Leaving me to drift down the greater torment of watching her flee her own confusion. And leaving me, while the bagel begins to smoke, with the deeper distress of realizing that, any longer, she does not know how to come back out from the bedroom to me and I do not know how to go in after her.

13

T he executive offices of the Bank of South Asia filled the
penthouse of a chrome-and-glass tower rising from the
foot of Battery Road on the edge of Singapore's harbour.

It was always as if the money possessed some kind of negative density or inverted gravity—the more you concentrated it, the higher it lifted its players to the upper reaches of office towers and condominium towers and hotel towers. As the quantity of money swelled, it lost its weight of coinage and bills. A room full of it could be evaporated into a string of zeros on a single bank draft, more flimsy than an airline ticket; a truck-load could be zapped around the world at the snap of a computer key.

Stepping out from the dizzying upward rush and spine-compressing halt of the high-speed elevator, I hesitated in the bank's airy foyer.

Broad two-storey-high windows sectioned up a panoramic view of the rows of cargo vessels baking on the brilliant water far below as they waited to enter the churned brown channels of the busy harbour. The darker ocean spread out, glassy, beyond them, and, in the steamy distance, the verdant islands of the Indonesian archipelago floated dreamlike along the lip of the South China Sea.

The bronze tinting of the glass turned patches of sunlight into a mottled pink carpet at my feet; the instability of the shimmering light on the marble floor taxing my limited reserves of balance.

I was reminded that, in non-stop travel, I had made poor trades of day for night without any rest, tropical heat for Canadian cold without sufficient fluids; I was now paying the price in exhaustion and dehydration.

My vision was jagged at its edges from fatigue.

I was jittery from harsh Asian coffee on an unsettled stomach.

I had arrived at midnight; plunged through a few hours sleep; risen, restless and unrested, out of ripples of jet lag at dawn; spent the early morning polishing off a pot of room service coffee, surfing CNN, repeatedly rehearsing this negotiation in my mind from a handful of different perspectives and likely outcomes; and had come directly to the bank's offices for their nine o'clock opening.

Still, now that I was here, I was more confident; my optimism returning from memory, fed by the headlong momentum of my travel and arrival, if by nothing else. In dashing halfway across the world without pausing for breath, I had given substance to my initiative and commitment; I had proved my willingness to go the distance. I was sustained also by my unflagging conviction that I was the only one who truly understood all of the complexities of the deal; like breath blown onto an ember to bring forth a glow, my seizing control of the bond issue would bring it back to vibrant success.

A final exhale to focus. I waded boldly across the swirling marble under the balls of my feet, pushed through the glass doors to the reception desk.

The receptionist grinned happily, recognizing me immediately, chirped a request into her telephone that, within several minutes, which we passed in courteous intermittent chatting, produced Albert Quan.

Balding, trim, tailored, Albert Quan was hurried in his handshake. "How very good to see you Mr. Smith." Then, without change in tempo, he added, "Were we expecting you? Our corporate finance group perhaps?"

"No," I stated evenly, "I came to see you. I flew twenty-six hours. Almost directly from our telephone discussion earlier this week."

"Then I had better not delay you any further." Albert Quan amply rounded up the tone of his response in feigned urgency to mitigate the inevitable confrontation lurking in our exchange.

Swimming upstream against my instincts and experience, towing my haggard sunrise rehearsal, I held my impatience in check as I followed Albert Quan down the hall to his office, declining refreshment as we seated ourselves in facing armchairs.

Crossing his ankles, leaning back slightly, Albert Quan opened with, "I very much hope that you are not expecting anything further on the Bangkok Commercial Bank bond deal."

"I am. And of course you know that."

"I thought I had made it very clear. That we both understood. That we closed that matter in our telephone conversation."

"We would like it re-opened."

Albert Quan was broadly avuncular, conciliatory. "Then I'm afraid you have come a very long way for nothing. There's nothing I can do. It's out of my hands. It fully belongs to Amsterdam Bank. We don't have the slightest role. We don't even have the slightest carried interest. I can do nothing."

Although I had hoped for some leverage in catching Albert Quan unprepared by my unannounced appearance, I had not expected it to shake him an ounce from his stance, and had counted on his intransigence to serve my arguments. Still, as I

measured the finality of his statements, the impending consequences of the demolished deal rushed up at me again. I struggled to hold my anxiety in check; and I found myself holding my
breath and grinding my molars in an attempt to curb my edgi-
ness and pace my delivery.

"I spent all yesterday afternoon with our attorneys here in
Singapore." I let the words of my lie dangle provocatively. "They
drafted our agreement with you. You know them."

Albert Quan's face clouded mildly, the corners of his mouth
tightened as he shrugged, bunching his crisp white shirt into
wrinkles across the top of his chest. "That's your prerogative."

"They say we can sue you for breach of contract."

"As I explained to you. We never signed any contracts."

"They have copies."

"We never passed a board resolution. Which is the only way
this bank can make a legally binding commitment to extend a
credit facility of that magnitude."

"We have your signature."

Albert Quan paused, stretched his fingers out in search
of some elusive word or thought. "Not a signature that I executed. Among other discrepancies in Stanley Man's files. As I
explained."

Although my simple half-lie had not reaped more effect, and
I had not expected it to succeed on its own, I was satisfied that
I had not been refuted or caught. I had succeeded in leading
Albert Quan to assume that, tomorrow if not yesterday, I could
bring our attorneys into the quarrel to increase my credibility
and my stature, compound my dispute.

"If this goes public," I stated, "in a big messy lawsuit for breach
of contract, even if we don't win, the negative press will turn
your shareholders against you and bring the Singapore regulators swooping down on you. Your board of directors will act the

same as any other board of any other bank. They'll cut you loose as soon as it goes sour and put as much distance between themselves and you as possible."

I did not have to convince him that it was possible; I only had to convince him I believed it was possible enough that I would attempt it.

More valuable was my floating of the allusion that I had stepped off the plane carrying the full authority of my firm to negotiate and act on their behalf, and that I wielded my firm's resources to support expensive litigation with unsure outcome in the courts. Implied in that was not the threat of lawsuit, but the threat that I would wield the money of my firm to protect myself in the same way that he was now using the money of his bank to protect himself. Leaving him, as Bank of South Asia's board of directors closed ranks against him, without a lifeboat.

My leverage flowing from always having an innate sense of the unwritten rules.

Deliberately, I waited, re-gathered my thoughts for my next attempt, listened to Albert Quan again verify that Stanley Mann was fraudulent, again confirm that the bank had the means and the inclination to menace me, letting him wind down into an expectant pause.

I let my reply spill out between us. "First you tell us that the loan contracts are fraudulent. Then you tell us that you've sold them to Amsterdam Bank."

"That's not what I said."

As soon as he wavered at the tail of his denial, I jabbed with a quick sharp demand. "Then what did you tell us?"

Albert Quan exerted visible effort to control his annoyance. "I said that we turned over our legal diligence and legal opinions on the bond offering to Amsterdam Bank because they agreed to reimburse us for our legal costs. Not contracts. Diligence and research. And opinions on the true value of the bonds, on the creditworthiness of the bank, and on the registration of the bonds under Thai securities regulations. You think it is cheap to create these legal asset-backed structures to take bonds into escrow before they've even been issued and lend money against collateral you don't even own yet?"

Instinctively, I followed his eyes, the way they strayed slightly off centre to the golf trophy clock on the wall, to the closed door. I could feel my stomach churn, hear it growl petulantly against the acidic coffee. I drew a stiff breath, leaned forward, interrupted his litany. "And what about the other concessions you got from Amsterdam Bank?"

"They paid the legal bills. What other?"

"There was more."

"Not that I know about."

"I think you do," I said.

"You heard what I told you."

"I don't think so."

He pulled his words together like loose ends of string. "You don't play golf, do you Mr. Smith?"

"No."

"I did not think so. You don't have any easy swing in you."

"You caved in."

"Caved in?"

"You did. The bank did. To Amsterdam Bank. Because they threatened to start dumping your stock. So you buckled under and handed over the deal to them, and reneged on your commitments to us."

Silence. Instant and total and wintry.

"No." Albert Quan's single syllable was imperative, and without indecision or hesitation.

With sudden respect, I recalculated Albert Quan's competence.

My own confusion, bottled within me, threatened to flare up as lament or rage.

Succinctly, I insisted, "You don't want to keep lying to me."

"I think, Mr. Smith, this meeting is over."

"I don't."

"I don't think we have anything to further discuss if you're only going to make unsupported allegations."

"And maybe they're not unsupported."

"Meaning?"

"Maybe I have access to certain files which support them. Certain internal memos regarding Amsterdam Bank."

Like clipping a brimming glass off the edge of the table and having the spill splash up from the floor before your mind registered the blunder and the impact.

Albert Quan narrowed his eyes, but ceded not an inch. "So," he mused, "this is how Stanley Man keeps his obligations. He's going to have a rude awakening when he finds our payments cut off and his accounts frozen."

Suspended in Albert Quan's dour remarks, I could sense him daring me to increase the level of aggression; and I could also somehow sense that I was too rapidly and too recklessly spending my shallow reserve of concentration. I had only my concentration left. I had nothing further to play. In going straight to my single piece of information of any substance, I had already overstepped the limits of Stanley's offer of assistance, exaggerated the value of Stanley's evidence, and had brought risk to Stanley's finances and professional references. How many more careless words to tip the scale from dishonesty to betrayal?

To decelerate, to dissipate some of the abrasion, I shook my head. Slowly. Wordlessly. Knowingly. I made a scornful gesture with the corner of my mouth. Making it clear that I was certain of my facts and that, with any further denial, Albert Quan would risk further exposure of his own falsehood and would surely humiliate himself.

Albert Quan was unyielding. "If this is what he wants, this is what he deserves."

"So you admit it's true. About Amsterdam Bank."

Albert Quan let his eyes slowly seek the ceiling, did not lower them; leaned back and slid his stiff fingers through his closely trimmed hair. "Mayfield Hotels."

"What does that mean?"

"You better ask Stanley Man."

"And what will he tell me?" I asked in prickly discord.

"If he's honest, he'll tell you that he brought us a deal from China Success Leasing, the owner of the Mayfield Group, for a quarter of a billion dollars worth of first mortgage bonds on twenty luxury hotel properties that Mayfield has from Seoul through to Kuala Lumpur."

Instinct advised me to wait for more.

"And if he's honest, he'll tell you that, when the real estate market collapsed in Tokyo a year ago and the collapse spread like wildfire throughout Southeast Asia, as you're well aware, our bonds were under-collateralized by almost fifty per cent in second position after the first mortgage holder, Mitsui Bank. And, as a result, we've had to take a provision for slightly more than a hundred million dollars."

I attempted to toss it off. "You and I both know that's a regular part of this business. When the commercial real estate markets bounce back your auditors will let you reverse the provision off your balance sheet."

"Be that as it may, Mr. Smith, knocking a hundred million off our value hit our share price hard the last quarter."

"You can't possibly blame Stanley Man for the state of the Asian real estate markets."

Albert Quan was crisp and precise in his explanation. "We don't want any new pressure on our share price this quarter from Amsterdam Bank. If that happens, someone outside our board of directors has to take the blame. Stanley Man will be found to have acted imprudently in promoting the Mayfield Hotel bonds. Sloppy in his diligence. Failing to provide us with a complete analysis of all contingencies."

"Why," I asked, "didn't you call the bonds at that point?"

"You and I both know the answer to that, Mr. Smith. We couldn't risk that the bonds might default. Singapore banking law is very strict. Very inflexible. If we forced a default of that magnitude, the Singapore regulators would demand half our directors resign for incompetence. Likewise, if Amsterdam Bank bleeds down our equity, it will be like the tide going out and leaving the error exposed on the beach. We would have to take a second hundred million provision, and the result with the regulators would be the same."

"And Stanley?"

"We'd see that he's formally charged. We'd have to."

"And you?"

"I would not be charged. But I'd be forced to resign."

"So you won't help me?"

"I cannot help you." Albert Quan rocked forward and brought his eyes and his words down with rebuke. "Admit that, in my position, you'd do the same and I'll know I'm talking with an honest man."

Reluctantly, resentfully, bitterly, I had to deliver a nod that was not a performance. I was intent on rescuing my money from similar calamity.

"Thank you." Albert Quan continued purposely. "Your group represents only a single corporate finance account. We have millions of depositors and shareholders we are responsible to. Are we to expose them to loss if we can possibly avoid it?"

"You're exposing them to our lawsuit."

Albert Quan would not bite on my argument, only fluttered his eyebrows and nibbled at the exposed edges of my logic. "You can sue us if you are foolish enough to believe your lawyers. But, even if you win, and we are forced to pay compensation and punitive damages, it will be a tiny fraction of what we would lose if our share value had been cut in half and our equity had dropped below reserve requirements. Besides, it will take you a year to get to court. Longer if we continually file for extensions. And, by that time, this bond deal will be issued, traded, and redeemed. Nothing left except trading records. Sue Amsterdam Bank instead and you'll be twice as long getting to court."

Unable to disagree, I could only refrain from agreeing by sitting without gesture or reply.

I calculated, in the face of Albert Quan's thorny denial, my options for salvaging my bonds, for redeeming myself and my career.

"What price would make it worthwhile?" Hastily, out of habit, I tried to shred my appeal into layers of negotiation and bargaining. "We could factor in some steep commissions for your sponsorship. Let's start by putting three per cent on the table."

"No." ·

"So you're just going to sit back and let Amsterdam make an example of us."

Nothing. My question dissolved as it loitered between us. In my frustration, I began to feel, in my tense knuckles and in my stiffening jaw, the clap of sweet rage to strike him. Or march out. Confront or flee, which would be more likely to save me?

I began pushing myself to my feet.

Sighing, Albert Quan leaned back, looked up to the ceiling as if searching for some window of deliverance.

I stayed. Sank back.

As I watched Albert Quan bring his face downward, I laboured to diminish the sounds of my breathing. Inside my head, I counted down the passing seconds, my inner voice always measuring what passed away from me.

Eventually, Albert Quan looked fully into my face with vague, moist eyes. "There's nothing we can do."

"Then refer me to another bank. So we don't have to start cold and spend a couple of months bringing the deal up to speed."

"You know that any other bank will only suspect the deal if we are passing it up. They will sense that something is wrong for us to let go of such a profitable deal. And I can't have that kind of attention and scrutiny upon us right now."

In his squint and tedious delivery, it was obvious how much Albert Quan detested the salt taste of lost respect and authority.

As our negotiation withered, I could feel the juices stirred up by our wrangling continue to swirl uselessly. I had expected Albert Quan and his bank directors to be adversaries to me, not adversaries to themselves. The threat of my lawsuit was dwarfed by the threat of loss and audit and investigation they had already hung over themselves.

Across from me, Albert Quan wearily pinged his fingernail against a bronze elephant paperweight that pinned down a neat stack of magazines on a carved table beside his chair. I followed the sound with my eyes; the glossy cover photograph of snowy Massachusetts trees stamped with a mailing label specifying his name in clean black ink; the bold blue masthead of the *Yale*

Alumni Magazine solidly supporting the elephant's broad flat feet.

There was no deal left to be made.

Without speaking further, I rose to leave Albert Quan's office.

Running on empty.

ᴔᴖ

Midday.

I pushed out into Singapore heat that came in swelling pulses, booming down from a naked sun. The heat soaked instantly into my neck and shoulders; it rose in a dancing shimmer off the concrete beneath my feet; and, at this hottest point in the day, it balled up in a pink haze at the end of each block. In the harbour, the humid sky met the water like sodden paper. A thick and tepid breeze barely rustled the heavy-hanging succulent leaves of the tropical plants and shrubs.

What the fuck now?

I walked the dozen blocks back to my hotel, sacrificing my sweat-spoiled shirt in an effort to deliberately insert an intermission into the runaway tempo of my thoughts. I required time to reorganize, to formulate my next actions. I had planned nothing beyond the urgent and immediate meeting with Albert Quan, expecting that the break in the chain could in some way be repaired at that link. Throughout my approach from half a world away, I had resisted the temptation of considering alternative possibilities to ensure that my single-minded pursuit of success was not needlessly dissipated. I had conserved my concentration, stubborn and miserly, not spending a spare thought, for the see-saw negotiations. Now the failed meeting hung on me like an unwanted coat. I toiled within my steps to reverse my polarity, seeking to absorb any possibilities, no matter how flimsy, from my reduced circumstances.

Bleary by the time I reached the hotel, as much from the heat as from the repercussions of Albert Quan's denial, I slogged past the hotel doorman, and was jolted as I hit a wall of interior air conditioning. The cold air was dry and flat and sharp-edged after the oily humidity of the street. Into its progressive layers of relief, and into the currents of movement and noise in the lobby, I advanced, disheartened in the poverty of my results, intent in my re-planning, lonely in my responsibilities.

Out of the milling confusion at the opposite end of the lobby, she surfaced. Standing at the reception desk.

I halted and watched her leaning against the counter. Speaking earnestly to a uniformed clerk. Her short hair was blue-black in the sudden clarity of the shivery air conditioning. Her navy suit jacket was bunched fiercely in her fist; her body, in a white blouse and navy skirt, was gently back-lit by the yellow light of the counter, lush in the bust and hips.

"Jesus," I mumbled.

It confused me to see her again; confused me more that, by the sight of her, I was halted short of the more pressing destinations, physical and emotional, in my life.

Still, I could not help hesitating, watching her; catching something inordinate in her hand gestures and the movement of her head as she spoke. Like anger. Or distress. Something. I did not know what. But enough that I began to walk toward her.

As I came closer, so that only billows of watery Muzak separated us, she snapped around conclusively.

I braked to a standstill, fumbling for an unexpected greeting.

Recognizing me, she demanded, "You have any pull at hotels in Singapore?"

"Afraid not," I answered, eager to shrug out a smile to give myself some anchorage. "Not my speciality. I don't handle real estate investment."

She grinned sternly. "Too bad."

"Trouble?"

"They've screwed up my booking," she explained. "Somehow got me checking out tonight when I need to stay until tomorrow."

"They can't switch you to another room?"

"Say they can't even switch me to another hotel. Some government summit's soaked up all the space. All they can do is give me a discount certificate for next time."

I faltered, failing to join her in some banter of criticism or complaint.

So she rapidly returned a strained smile to break off our encounter. "I'd better go make some calls in a hurry."

Her words were guarded, meant to maintain a distance between us; making me regret that I had approached her across this lobby hoping to retouch the flickers of friendship from our flight.

She frowned down at her clutch of hotel invoices and receipts for some solution to her problem. When she looked up, she became aware I had remained.

Now I was embarrassed to be standing there, watching her. Feeling awkward, not knowing what else to say, I told her feebly "Hope you have better luck with your calls than you had with the hotel."

She made some careless unbiased gesture with her hands.

I hoped her preoccupation with her own concerns prevented her from sensing my loss of balance, my lack of direction.

"Hope everything works out," I told her, relieved that her distraction allowed me to extricate myself without having to make tenuous excuses. I sensed I needed to conserve everything I had left to cope with Albert Quan's duplicity.

Gratefully, I retreated into the cacophony of passing conversations swirling up around us. I tried to collect my diluted focus by concentrating on the resonance of my breathing, on the crackling of the leather soles of my shoes on the polished marble as I launched myself across the lobby. The sound and momentum triggered deeply rooted habits. I checked my watch, started to hurry, and actually searched my thoughts for a list of appointments before I caught myself and corrected my pace to the circumstance of an empty outcome and vacant afternoon.

I held back.

Are there times when you lose your emotional horizons, leaving your heart to navigate by nothing more than faint beacons of desire?

I reeled back around to her, spilling words into the orbit of my turn. "What about my room?"

She raised her eyebrows. Brightened. Picked it up eagerly. "How so?"

"I'm booked in here for another two days. But I can go on to Bangkok early."

"Your plans have changed?"

"I've just decided." Best to find out immediately if the directors of Bangkok Commercial were still aligned with me, or whether they also had been smothered by Amsterdam Bank.

"I'll check out," I explained. "Get them to give you my room."

"That's very generous. Thank you."

"Not at all. Come on."

I pivoted, returned to the counter without having to confirm that she accompanied me.

The clerk listened politely, smiling throughout. Then replied by explaining," I'm very sorry, sir. But we can't do that. Our policy is that all vacant rooms must be offered to people on our waiting list. And there are at least thirty or forty people ahead of this lady on our list."

I wavered, unsure how to play it.

"I'll be pleased to have the shift manager speak with you," the clerk offered in a properly mannered interception of any dispute or any gain in our voice levels.

I hesitated, feeling empty-handed. Two worthless negotiations in one day.

To go further away or to come back; what makes us decide?

"No. That's okay," I stated, cropping off any further response from the clerk. "I've changed my mind. I'll stay. I'll keep my room as booked."

The clerk nodded conclusively. "Very well sir."

I eased away from the counter, turned and touched her arm to have her keep pace with me. As we pulled out of the clerk's periphery, I suggested, "Come up to 1201 in a minute. I'll explain."

She nodded.

We separated.

In the several minutes it took before she knocked on the door, I had pulled out my luggage and packed off my bathroom counter.

I let her in.

She stood at the foot of the bed, dabbed the sleeve of her bunched suit jacket against the perspiration above her eyes.

"I'm leaving now," I told her. "I'll give you my key. Move your stuff up here and you'll be okay."

"What about your check-out?"

"I won't check out at the front desk. They'll just automatically assume I used express check-out, charge everything to my credit card, and mail me a copy of the bill."

"And how will I pay you?"

"Give me your business card. I'll send you a copy of the bill. You can send a cheque."

She hesitated, edgy, tentative. "You sure?"

Reaching into my closet for some shirts, I risked some gentle humour. "You're not good for it?"

Barely, she smiled. "I was just figuring out how our accounting department will look at it."

"If they don't pay, don't worry about it. Be a drop in the bucket against what I've lost here today."

She let it pass. Dug a business card from an inside pocket of her jacket. "Here."

I flipped it into my open briefcase. Worked around her, hanging suits and shirts into my folding suit-bag. As much for proficient display as to effect the task at hand. Pushing it into a gesture larger than a simple favour, pushing the pace of it into a race to reach the airport beyond the simple requirement of re-booking my flight. I was eager to taste the satisfaction derived from playing outside the rules. After the deep disappointment of Albert Quan's office, something, somehow, was owed to me. And I was going to collect no matter how trifling.

It only served to unsettle her; she fidgeted her heels into the carpet.

So I asked politely, "How's your other stuff going?"

"Fine," she shrugged, indifference in her lopsided shoulders.

I nodded, turned away from her and away from the trembling breeze of the air conditioning, zipped my bags before she could change her mind, hefted them to the door, feeling the heat of my exertion beginning to paste itself to my face.

I fished out my room key, handed it to her.

"Where you going to be in Bangkok?" she asked. "You could be handy."

I sensed that her words were strung together with loose attitude; her discomfort with her dependence on my assistance had
overcome her gratitude; she was not sincere.

I did not answer.

14

When I arrive home from Bangkok a week after we arrive home from Nassau she has been dead for a night and a day.

She is lying on our bed, wearing familiar sleep attire that insists everything is normal, a turquoise knee-length jersey T-shirt with a crest on the pocket boasting "It's Better in the Bahamas."

A crocheted comforter over her legs. Now unneeded to her cold blue feet.

Her hands are loose at her sides. Unforgiving in that they neither comfort nor conceal her, but leave her body exposed to the finality of what she has done.

And her head is rolled over onto one cheek facing away from the bedroom door, as if she is shamed by my presence.

There is no evidence of her raging emotional struggle, only evidence of her final desperate decision in a small crusted clot of dried vomit on the pillowcase, yellow-brown.

On the night table beneath a lamp still burning, one empty plastic vial that had contained Luvox from this month's prescription, another that has been depleted of a handful of Effexor left half finished since Easter.

And a note of sorts that she has written in her looping script with a purple felt pen across the cover of the TV Guide: "sorry."

A single word to encompass her suicide.

Its echo, and its endless regret, left to slosh forward and back in the abandoned circumstances of her life, and spilling over into mine. Forever.

The weight of my undeposited luggage begins to strain my fingers and wrist, yet I am incapable of setting it down—as if I have arrived by mistake at the wrong destination and must straightaway turn around and leave.

Looking at her body, I do not see her dead, only distanced and removed from me.

Looking at her, bluntly mindful she will never hear my last words for her, I taste the terror of my days to come, spiralling out, without her, through all of the time remaining in my life.

For an instant, I recall some long-forgotten grade school play: jiggling in the dusty curtains of an auditorium stage in a hand-sewn costume with words blowing inside my head like a snow-storm, trying to tame my urgent bladder, the birds of similar anguish feeding on my guts.

Loss fills me as if it is being poured into me from a pitcher, flooding me to the brim, overflowing out of me and spilling into the empty spaces of the room.

The words of a song crowd into my head and weakly leave my lips, "Love has gone."

The sparse words seem to break apart and evaporate into the immensely still air of the bedroom before they can reach my ears.

15

B angkok.

Fuck!

I remained as still as possible in the bed, not allowing my eyes to drift left or right off the dissolving shadows on the ceiling, hoping that some alchemy in the ritual would return me to my brief dream. But it was no use. The immense jet lag of a twelve-hour time difference pulled within me like a riptide, left me twitchy and restless. Dry-mouthed.

I rolled from the tangled sheets, stepped naked to the window, and bunched back a handful of curtain.

Dawn. A feathery resonance of grey and yellow light stained with pink haze.

Five floors below me, on the four lanes of Rama iv Road, one of the primary thoroughfares cutting south to north through Bangkok, the traffic had already built to a crammed mass of tooting vehicles emitting clouds of exhaust that would rise into a sticky brown smog and drift out to carpet the entire city within another hour.

In the immense Lumpini Park across the street, joggers huffed along the tracks and, on the baked-down grass, old men slowly breathed their way through the gentle, graceful forms of their morning tai chi.

As I let the curtain drop, I noticed the damp, mouldy condensation at the edge of the window sash that stained the wallpaper and caused it to curl back off the plaster. These stains, wherever the interior air conditioning and the exterior heat leaked into each other, I recognized everywhere in the cities of Southeast Asia. Even in the billion-dollar business towers and the five-star hotels like this one, no amount of technology could ever fully subdue the climate's natural furnace of scalding heat and humidity.

I reached to the chair where I had dropped my clothes, pulled on my jeans, yesterday's sour shirt. Ordered coffee and toast from room service. When it came within minutes, I sat on the corner of the messy bed, sipping the potent coffee. I began marking up pages on a yellow legal pad, a habitual process of trying to think my way through to a solution by drawing out everything I knew, everything I deduced and inferred, in words, scribbles, numbers, doodles, and diagrams. I filled a page with a triangle at its centre, with lopsided circles capping each point of the triangle, the names of the players printed in the three circles: BNGK COMMERCIAL BNK...BNK SOUTH ASIA...US DOING THE DEAL...clusters of numbers estimating bond sales and profits, becoming smaller and more crimped, with the zeros bumping into each other as they ran out of space on the right edge of the page...lines and arrows plunging into AMSTERDAM BNK...chains of blue dots linking WE FAIL FUNDS...to ATLANTIC LAURENTIDE...GLOBAL VEST-BAHAMAS...other pages littered with scribbled notes for courses of action, contained in balloons connected by a cradle of strings in an attempt to organize them by priority...the first few items in a stubby list of things to do today, each announced by a scratchy star...

YALE...scored by a square around the four steep letters, digging a rut into the page with my pen to drag a second square around the first, a third square around the second.

"Shit."

It comes to me in degrees, and incomplete. Still, it brings a sense of my old magic, of my being exempt from bad luck; and an anticipation of having the final stretch of my failed actions taper to a close, freeing my future to second chances.

With great care not to interrupt the positive vibrations, I rested the pad on the lumpy bedspread, swivelled to the telephone.

Michelle answered, chatty and cheerful.

"I was just grabbing my coat to leave, Mr. Smith. It's almost six o'clock. What time is it there?"

"Just coming up to six in the morning."

"Good lord. Are you working on that big Chinese deal?"

"You bet. Is Molly still there?"

"Already left."

"When do you leave for your holiday?"

"Tomorrow's my last day."

"Could you do me a favour and stay a little late tomorrow?"

"We're all going for drinks after work."

"Just ten minutes."

"I guess so."

"Can you talk to Molly tomorrow? In private. Don't tell anyone else. Not Kyle. Get her to give you a file off her computer called 'Global Vest Banking Corporation.' In Bahamas. With her password."

"Is that all?"

"Download the file after she leaves tomorrow night. But don't email it to me. I don't want any record of it on our email server. Fax it to me at this hotel. You've got the numbers in my travel file. Then delete your download. Delete your fax. Delete everything. So nobody ever knows you sent it. Not Molly. Not Kyle. Not anybody. Okay?"

"Why is it so secret?"

"It's just really important that it be this way right now."

"Are you sure this is okay?"

"Yes."

"I need to stay out of trouble. This vacation has wiped out my savings. I can't afford to look for a new job right now."

"This may be the one thing that saves your job."

"How?"

"It may be the one thing that saves the firm."

"But you said the firm wasn't in trouble."

"It's not. As long as you send me that file."

"I'm not so sure."

"Just please trust me. I'll make sure there's no trouble."

"Okay, Mr. Smith. I'll do the best I can. I've always trusted you."

As I let the receiver, half heavier with my half lies, roll off my fingers, I could feel the flux of caffeine burst into a ripple of sweat along my brow, hear it sizzling in my ears. Parts of myself that I could not identify by touch were peeling back like the wallpaper, exposing the rawness I kept concealed beneath. And I could sense a spiking in my adrenaline, and in the motion and acceleration of my thoughts, as if I had unexpectedly leaned too far out of an open window.

I began to defy everything, even the empty air, to now make demands on me.

వావు

On previous occasions, I have been seduced by immersion in the delirious pace of commerce in Bangkok. Even fuelled by it.

The money turning on a word or a nod in days running without break dawn to dawn. Yet this afternoon, dragging my baggage of bad news from Singapore, sidelined to an empty chair in the corner of an empty waiting room, waiting on someone else's schedule for a meeting that has become my lifeline, the day has been sluggish. The hours of waiting had soaked up my stamina, left my attention span shortened and my thoughts shallow by the time Sanoh Sajjakul stepped off the elevator and ushered me into his office.

Despite my anxious focus, Sanoh Sajjakul's managing director's office at Bangkok Commercial Bank was oddly comforting in its familiarity, ringed with waist-high rubbery plants potted in deep ceramic urns, and crowded with traditional carved mahogany furniture on clawed feet, ponderous and polished—antiques from distant generations when the bank had been a place for the tallying of crumpled notes and dingy coins behind locked doors. An official portrait of the king on the wall behind the oversized desk; an inscribed photo of a famous Buddhist scholar lower along a side wall. An intricately carved jade bridge under glass on a cumbersome corner table. The space was sliced throughout by slanting bands of afternoon sunlight, molten with smog, streaming through the dusty slats of the vertical blinds as the sinking sun caught the upper floors of the office tower.

Sanoh Sajjakul backed himself into a wide chair. His jowls shadowed with grey-and-white beard, his damp-stained white shirt, straining across the fat rolls of his chest and stomach, and the knot of his tie slackened to half mast were a portrait of his long hot day.

"I'm sorry," he began, "that you were kept waiting so long, Mr. Smith. We were not expecting you. I was out on the coast inspecting a dry-dock facility we are financing. Only sixty kilometres away," he lifted his open palms to emphasize the obvious, "but, as you know, many hours with our dreadful traffic jams." He settled back decisively into his chair. "Welcome. Thank you for waiting. Now, how may I help you?"

As much as I had reviewed my details for this meeting, and rehearsed their nimble presentation during the tedium of waiting out the first part of the afternoon in the ground-floor coffee shop and the final part in the waiting room, I found it difficult to spur myself to sufficient velocity of concentration and performance. Jet lag that reversed night and day, and only a few quick grabs at sleep in the last forty-eight hours, betrayed my vigorous ambition; and I felt as if I was having to think between gaps in my brain and invent each word before I spoke it.

I swallowed slackly. "We need to discuss a few developments on the bond deal."

"Of course," Sanoh Sajjakul insisted. "Our bonds."

"I need to know if you're aware of any problems?"

"I should hope not. Those bonds are being used to securitize a lot of dormant real estate assets and take them off our balance sheet."

"We're fully aware of that."

Sanoh Sajjakul continued, edging up his momentum and emphasis. "With all the clamping down by the International Monetary Fund and insistence by our own central bank that we push our reserves back up to eight per cent, we just made it under the wire of last year's deadline to get that bond offering approved. We'd never get approved now. We'd never meet the newly imposed capital adequacy requirements."

"Would the central bank let you reduce the amount? Divide it into two or three smaller deals that could be sold off more easily?"

"No new approvals. No new deals. Not for us. We'd never

meet the capital adequacy ratio with the way the IMF has jacked up the new limits to meet the Basel II Accords."

I continued trying. "Would the central bank let you have any extension for closing this bond offering over a longer period of time if it took us longer to complete all the selling? A couple of extra months?"

"Never. The central bank jumps at every chance it gets to curtail bank borrowing in this country and bring the reserves back up." Sanoh Sajjakul leaned forward, restated his single word as if he were placing it on deposit and requesting a receipt. "Never."

Our conversation closed in on itself around the inarguable repetition of this negative obstacle, prematurely cutting off any alternative routes of discussion. We sat in a stillness swelling up out of the sighing of the air conditioning, amplified by the silence of surrounding offices now empty at end of day and by the creeping dimness of the weakening sunlight. Each of us waiting for the other to be the first to concede.

Too poor in stamina for subtleties, I wagered my remaining capacity on a direct question, propelling it with the impoliteness of a direct stare. "Have you heard from Amsterdam Bank?"

"No."

"I think you have," I claimed crisply.

The exaggerated courtesy and the restraint of voice and gesture mandatory in the conduct of Asian business meetings boiled away in my dry contradiction and its allegation of perjury.

Sanoh Sajjakul scratched at the flaky crown of his scalp, centred his buttocks in his chair, declared blandly, "They say you can't pay."

"And what else?"

"They're offering cash."

"How much?"

"Enough."

"As much as we contracted to pay you?"

"I'm not quite sure of the exact figures." Sanoh Sajjakul submitted his disclosure with no crack in his conviction, leaving no tolerance for any contention.

Yet, sensing that I now had little further to fall to reach solid ground beneath me, I threw off his statement with a slight twist of my head. "You're sure of them. Very sure of them."

"I am?"

"If you've gone with Amsterdam, you know all the numbers in your sleep at this point."

Folding his jaw down into the rolls of his chin, Sanoh Sajjakul sucked phlegm to the back of his throat. "Our contract with you calls for you to buy the bonds from us at a discount of eight per cent. You pay us ninety-two cents on the dollar. Correct?"

"Of course."

"Ninety-two million for the entire offering of one-year maturity bonds with a face value of one hundred million."

"Yes."

"Except," Sanoh Sajjakul repeated with emphasis, "Amsterdam Bank is telling us that your financing has fallen apart."

"Not necessarily."

"And they're offering us cash."

"But," I stressed, "if they know you're in trouble, they'll be gouging for blood."

"They'll buy the entire bond offering. Immediately."

"But how much less?"

"We can't afford not to close these bonds."

"Can you afford that much blood?"

"If we don't sell the bonds and we don't move the real estate debt off our balance sheet, we'll fail to meet reserve requirements. And the central bank will take us over. Put us on the auction block. By year end."

I leaned forward, converging on the critical information. "How much below ninety-two are they offering?"

"They say," Sanoh Sajjakul confessed, "that the market is ninety-two. And that they've already pre-sold all our bonds. Sold them all out below market at ninety-one or ninety and three-quarters."

"And what are they offering you. Ninety and a half?"

Squeezing his sides with his thick fingers, Sanoh Sajjakul paused. Reticent. Stubbornly hesitant. Then admitted, "They're offering us eighty-seven flat."

"Eight-seven? Flat?"

"Immediate cash. Take it or leave it."

"A spread of four points. They're gouging you for four million dollars and change just to flip your bonds?"

"And? Your financing? Better? Certainly not if it's fallen apart and you don't have it for us."

"They're only going to flip your bonds by dumping them below market. You never would have signed those terms with us. You know that's wholesale slaughter."

"You don't have the financing. After you promised it to us. Guaranteed it to us in writing. What choice do we have?"

As I was about to spring forward with my response, I lost my grip on my thoughts. I could feel them dropping down a deep well of unknowns and uncertainties that kept each solution clouded; leaving me frantic to reach out and save them. I squirmed in my chair, searching for a position that would keep my concentration from fading out, keep the fatigue from swooping down behind my eyes. The exertion and movement only made me feel as if my eye sockets had become too large, leaving my eyes loose and unguided in lassitude. No longer able to focus on the urgent items laid out in front of me.

I knew a solution. All afternoon I had kept a single important thought from straying, herding it like a wayward animal, penning it in to be released at the proper moment. I clawed up the closest word of my thought, appraised it, discarded it for lacking impact. Pulled up the next word in the chain. Working my way to the key word.

I licked my lips.

Finally blurted, "Non-transferable."

"What," Sanoh Sajjakul demanded, "our bonds?"

"Yes."

"And who would hold them if they couldn't be transferred? Couldn't be resold?"

"Amsterdam Bank would not be able to flip them as planned. So they would not be able to buy them."

"No."

"You'd cut them off."

"And cut our own throats."

"Not if we raised the financing to hold them to maturity."

"You have no financing."

"I can get it." Pledging results so far in advance of my actions, I felt shaky and light-headed as I soared up into an atmosphere where the air between promise and deception was so thin I could not breathe it. "If you can do it."

"It would have to be approved by our board of directors. They would only vote for it if you could prove you had the funds in hand."

"Can you give me a day or two?"

Sanoh Sajjakul shrugged, round-shouldered. Frowned. "Legally. No. But there is some time because everything will be very confused for the next few days. Because we have to obtain legally binding notification from your firm that the deal is in jeopardy. Amsterdam Bank know that we can not legally deal with them until we have verification of breach from your firm."

I tried to continue it, to urge it up the steep slope of renegotiation, all the while struggling to push my spilled thoughts back into line. Stalled.

"So." Sanoh Sajjakul closed off his attention as if he were closing a book, hefted himself to his feet. "If that is as far as it can go for now, let me compensate you for your long wait by taking you to dinner. We can discuss the terms and concessions you would have to make to us."

I could only follow obediently.

めべ

The elevator plummeting down to the ground floor of the bank tower. In unison, we stepped out, crossed the lobby, and were let out by a security guard onto the muggy dark street. A small battered Toyota cab picked us up at the curb. The back seat lopsided with Sanoh Sajjakul's bulk and burden, we beetled insanely through clouds of acrid exhaust, blaring horns, and a bumping river of vivid tail-lights. To Pat Pong, the nightclub and brothel district. Pat Pong's special street blocked off and restricted solely to pedestrian traffic. Like some exotic carnival dedicated to sex, staged in an exempted place where everyone was certain that God, East or West, was not watching too closely. We elbowed down an X-rated midway of babbling crowds cruising the blocks of flashy clubs, all touting deafening rock music, free-flowing liquor, raw live-sex shows, and legions of prostitutes. Into a wide pink restaurant with many rows of tables. Bathed in a fusion of multi-coloured fluorescent light. Smokey. A smell of garlic and curry and sour beer as thick as velvet. Loud to the point where I could feel the fuzzy thump of the music in my spine as much as I could hear it blare off the walls and ceiling.

Throughout it all, I lurched along at Sanoh Sajjakul's heels, laden with exhaustion, physical and emotional and mental, as if I was moving my limbs underwater, listening with cotton stuffed in my ears, speaking with stones in my mouth.

I felt a failure to be begging my bonds back together. And heartbroken in small places.

Platters of food appeared, filling our table to all edges with plates of glassy-eyed fish, wavy lemon grass, plump spicy noodles, pad Thai with slivers of vegetables and pork stir-fried in coconut milk, steaming mounds of fragrant rice.

Although hungry from having eaten sparingly throughout the day, I only plucked bits of food with my chopsticks. Chewed without tasting. Gentle pulses of nausea looped within me like a snake eating its own tail.

Across from me Sanoh Sajjakul shovelled it down. Speaking with his mouth full. In English, as he urged the food on me, outlined his requirements for swinging his board of directors over to converting the bond offering to non-transferable bonds, and proclaimed his strategies for getting the central bank to buy off on the conversion by creating an unbreakable succession of interlocking trusts to connect the bonds to the underlying real estate assets. In shrill sputters of Thai, as he placed orders with waitresses, directed the delivery of the food, and fielded calls on his cell phone.

Straining to keep up with the vast scope of Sanoh Sajjakul's ideas, with the breakneck pace of his deal development and construction, and with his staggering attention to detail, I was solidly reminded that, in addition to a banking career that included stints with the Thai government's Ministry of Finance, the man was also a respected professor of economics at the country's leading university and was regularly appointed by the World Bank to its Asian finance committees. And, despite all of the habitual connotations of sloth so often ascribed to obesity, he was my most dynamic and potent ally on this side of the world.

I struggled to keep my attention screwed to the torrent of details, constantly nodding to mask my snarled perception.

In my mind, I saw Michelle's yard sale. The paper bond certificates piled up in a dense stack on her battered yard sale table under the Saturday afternoon sun, the edges of the green certificates fluttering in the summer breeze. Me standing there in my faded sweat shirt and ratty running shoes, offering to pay nine dollars for the bonds so I could resell them for ten dollars. Keep the extra dollar in a jar on my kitchen counter.

Eventually, as the first of the dishes began to be cleared away, Sanoh Sajjakul sat back, wound down his discourse, let his cell phone drop to the table, wiped at his chins with a wad of paper napkins, belched behind his hand politely. "I think we are agreed on the fundamentals."

Gratefully, I nodded, stuffing my memory with crucial details. Panic-driven by the fresh work heaped up by our negotiation.

"Look there," Sanoh Sajjakul ordered, flipping his fingers across the table.

As directed, I twisted around in my chair to look behind me.

Next to a bottle-cluttered bar, doe-eyed girls sat in a row of chairs along one wall. High school age, by my estimate. Their hands in their laps. All of them dressed in limp, wrinkled, pastel silk ball gowns. And in high heels. With blue plastic number tags hung around their slender necks on silk ribbons. Each a different number. All of them lavishly bored, gazing out vapidly, tapping their scuffed high heels to the beat of the Thai rock music. Sounding out the words to the repetitive trilling tunes from lips caked with cracked lipstick.

As I swivelled back to the table, Sanoh Sajjakul called out in Thai, something quick and short and pointed.

Two of the girls stepped in towards the table and slid around into his periphery where he engaged them in a chopped exchange of words and nods.

Finishing, Sanoh Sajjakul grinned at me fiercely. "Pick one. I'll take the other. It will be charged to the dinner on my expense account."

In a diluted reflex, I lifted my palms an inch above my half-full plate. "Thank you. But it's not necessary."

"Are you married?" Sanoh Sajjakul asked.

I floundered, unsure if I now was or not. "No."

"Then this is good for you."

"Please."

"Very safe. They will give you the best condoms."

I faltered, shrugged it away with what I hoped was a polite and appreciative smile.

"Good for us," Sanoh Sajjakul advised heartily. "Good for our business. Good for our bonds."

Afraid to protest further for fear it might unravel our negotiation on the bonds, with some vague idea that this issue would be easier to resolve when I was distanced from Sanoh Sajjakul's jovial insistence, I pointed to the closest girl.

She took my lifted hand, pulled kindly, eased me up from my chair, led me around the edge of the bar, and motioned with her cupped fingers for me to follow her up some stairs. At the top, a few steps along a short hallway. Into a dim room. Cramped. With only a bed and a sink and a chair. Neon light from the street pulsing in through the ratty curtains of the narrow window. On the chair, a plastic bowl identical to the one containing rice on the restaurant table, this one brimming with shiny packages of condoms. A separate feast for separate appetites.

She closed the door.

I became aware of the discoloured wallpaper and the mouldy damp air conditioning.

I did not know what to say; how to say it; I had assimilated only minimal Thai: hello, and please, and thank you.

Without prelude, she kicked her high heels under the edge of the bed. Unzipped the ball gown. Stepped from it. Her breasts swung like little beanbags. She reached to a hanger clacking from a nail on the back of the door, slipped it into the gown, and hung the deflated gown onto the nail in a gesture that seemed to me practised and familiar and matter-of-fact, and devoid of any mystery or feeling, as if hanging clothes she had just washed.

She snapped off her panties.

"What do you want?"

She was the first woman I had seen naked since the last time I had seen Judith naked.

How long ago? I spoke the question within myself so abruptly I could not tell if I had also pronounced it out loud. My vision flickered as I spun some mental calendar.

"Fuck or blow job?" She shifted her weight onto one hip pertly. Her breasts jiggled.

Since the moment I discovered her dead, I have had a constantly present thought of Judith; a circular thought of Judith living and dying that seemed to be attached to my inhaling and exhaling. In this first time of truly realizing that, along with my wife's personality, her body was also forever absent from my life now, I relived her death repainted in gaudy carnal memories that had been banished by her funeral and church service and flowery cards of condolence. In knife-like flashes of Judith laying herself open and clenching at orgasm, I foundered anew on jagged recall of how her abundant sexual hunger had withered within the cruel drought of her depression. Like a light taken farther and farther away and fading into distant obscurity. I had not been able to talk of it with her, nor utter my frustration of our lost lovemaking, of my derelict lust, as I had watched it happen to her. How could I? She was sick. What kind of husband could be that selfish? It was our unspoken horror. Never discussed between us. Never discussed with friends. But always looming near whenever we were together, our bodies proximate in the same room.

I stared deeply at the prostitute's dusky nipples. At the fleshy lips of her labia. And layers of emotion that I had kept stubbornly suppressed rose to connect me with the loss of my wife.

"What's wrong?" she demanded.

The revived pain of Judith's death was so acute it severed me from my language to describe it. When I tried to utter it outside my thoughts, the words tore away from my voice like meat torn from the skin of the crispy duck I had just eaten. Imprisoned within me, with no words to facilitate its release, the pain flooded up around me like a moat. I was incarcerated within it because I had no ability to describe it. Devoid of language, I was reduced. Mute. Suffering. Driven by a compulsion to burrow beneath the layers of my life for solace and escape and relief.

"No more waiting," she insisted.

I looked into her face. Where did she come from, this girl? How did she do this over and over again? What will become of her? I did not even know her name.

"What's your name?" I asked.

She shrugged off my question impatiently; get to the business at hand; get the money; get back downstairs for the next customer.

I was shot through with heartbreak at how her life was made up from the scraps left from someone else's plate.

"I give you blow job." She knelt, began to dig at my belt and zipper.

I pushed her away.

She popped back up to her feet. Indignant. "Fuck you. Asshole..."

I pulled a fistful of Thai baht notes from my pocket. Pressed them into her hand. Shouldered by her to leave the room and go back downstairs.

"Not tonight," I mumbled.

16

Closing time for my brain.

Shuttling blindly back to my hotel in the taxi, the dense tropical night folded around me like a fist. I broke from the humid darkness into the throbbing lights of the lobby, intent on reaching my room and the numbing void of sleep.

"You look like death warmed over."

I stepped headlong into the comment halfway to the elevators.

My instinctive shrug, a forgery I have been employing at the office to shield myself by implying that I am preoccupied with larger issues, faltered.

I followed the thread of her voice to bring her face into focus. I said, "Hello."

"You're here?"

"Yes. You're here, too?"

"Yes. I triple-checked my reservation this time."

I knew it was relevant, but did not want to spend fresh effort to make any further connection to ideas or people. The day seemed unending.

"Don't worry," she explained, "I won't bump you out of your room."

I sensed that a grin was the correct response; I made every effort.

"So," she said, "we meet again. Surprise."

"Indeed. So nice to see you." I was pleased, but did not know how to rise above my exhaustion. "Sorry I'm so bagged out from jet lag."

She nodded. "Tell me about it."

This second comment caused me to glance beyond her to the elevators, their digital numbers bubbling like bees, my room waiting above.

"Thank you again, by the way. That was very nice of you in Singapore. Although I never expected we'd end up at the same hotel here."

"Neither did I."

"Just back from dinner?" she asked.

"Sort of."

"Same. I should buy you that drink. Staying in Singapore yesterday was important. We had a lot of recent research to review. It added some critical findings to our presentation for this conference."

"I think I'll have to take a rain check."

"I think I'd have to agree. You look awful."

"Feel worse than that."

"Got any Tylenol?"

"No." I had always depended on Judith to slip some medication into my packing.

"Come on."

Without speaking further, she whisked me up to her floor, led me down the corridor to her room. Inside, all the lights were on. The table and chairs were covered in sheaves of paper. The backs of the chairs were balled with layers of clothes. A pair of black pumps hung by their heels from the open door of the television cabinet. I sat where she pointed, on a space at the bottom of the bed.

She came out of the bathroom with two pills in her palm, took a bottle of water from the mini-fridge. "Any nausea?"

"Some."

"That's okay, these are coated."

She trickled the two pills into my hand; twisted the cap on the bottle to crack the plastic seal and handed it out. "Down the hatch."

I flipped the pills onto my tongue, tipped the bottle, swallowed. Strangely, I discovered I was thirsty and kept lifting the bottle to sip at the frosty water.

"Jet lag, and this heat, can really take the stuffing out of you," she agreed without me having to say it.

"Killing me this time around," I confessed. "I've only knocked off a couple of naps in the last two days. Like going half a week without sleep."

"Stay awake for another hour or so, at least until ten o'clock. If you force your body over the hump to local time, you won't keep waking up at three in the morning, and you can get a decent night's sleep and get back on your feet."

"Don't seem to be able to this trip."

"Sit here for a little while. Keep talking to stay awake. I owe you that much. Besides I need to do the same thing."

"Okay." I remained sitting on the edge of the bed, feeling, as my pace slowed, the tension that had collected into stiffness across my shoulders and in the muscles of my calves and thighs.

She cleared a stack of papers from a chair, dropped down, swung her heels onto the edge of the low coffee table, revealing a flash of pale ankles in her loose slacks, slumped back. "Well, Paris Smith, you already know what I do. What do you do?"

"Money."

"Money?"

"Banking and investments."

"Where?"

"Here. Back there. Lot of other places. I go wherever the money goes."

"Is it like they make it out to be in television and the movies, chasing the money? Selling your soul for something soul-less? Lots of dramatic negotiations with lots of sex appeal and luxury in the process?"

"It's not the money, it's what you build with it."

"And what's that like?"

"Most of the time it's relentless. It never stops, never lets you rest. There's always a place in the world where the sun is high and the money is moving, and there's not an ounce of compassion if you close your eyes. But sometimes it's more seductive than sex. Sometimes, when you get it right, hit it dead centre, it's like painting."

"That's rather poetic."

"Everyone thinks it's about chasing after dollars. But it's not. Sometimes you can identify two opportunities in two different places. And, if you can paste them together with the right investment, you'll manufacture success. It's like seeing what is on the blank canvas before the money is added to the picture. And that's what you have to concentrate on, the finished picture. Or you'll never get the money. That's what most people, who chase after the dollars out of greed or fear, never understand. And that's why they fail."

"And you don't fail."

"Not," I said, "very often."

"Because it's like painting for you."

"Like painting." Then I saw the genuine interest in her eyes when I least expected it and felt I owed her more. "But it's also like your brushes are dipped in fire. You always have to go very fast, because if you don't stay ahead of the game and stay in one place too long, you can burn up the opportunities, have them lose their value, the money goes elsewhere, your deal doesn't close, and you come away with nothing."

My energy for further explanation ran out.

We sat silent. I drank more water.

She asked, "How'd you get stuck with Paris?"

"My mother was a high school history teacher. She thought I needed something heroic to go with Smith."

"Did you?"

"Perhaps. But I don't think she allowed for locker room nicknames on the basketball team."

She chuckled.

She moved on by asking, "What made you sail in and give up your room like that? I mean, after I turned you down on the plane."

Any agile reply was dragged down by headache and fatigue. "You had been kind to me on the plane. I was sure you thought I'd repaid you by coming on to you. Some jerk." I crumbled back onto one elbow. "I really didn't want you to think that about me. That I was interested in you like that."

"Why not?"

"Because I was interested in you for something more than that."

"Obviously."

Her reply resonating between us, I looked down at my fingers, swollen from the heat and splayed across the quilted pattern of the rumpled bedspread, deliberately taking her out of my view so that I did not have to face the reprimand in her knowing, in her flattened smile.

She sighed to put it behind us. Persisted. "Only other thing I know is that you told me you lost someone recently. I've reached the age where I've started to go through parent's funerals with family and friends. You?"

"My mother a couple years ago."

"And your father?"

"Still going strong. Sold the house. Retired south near Jacksonville."

"See him much?"

"Not really." I recited it. "We get along okay. But not much to talk about. My dad was a civil servant all his life. A lawyer with the Ministry of Immigration. We used to joke about having to get our passports stamped when he came home for dinner every night. Pensioned out after thirty years. He doesn't have any understanding of the financial stuff I do. Or the entrepreneurial deal-making part."

She raised her arms, laced her fingers behind her neck, stretched in tiredness. "Who's we?"

"My older sister."

"Not her funeral recently?"

"No."

"How's it with her?"

It was beginning to take too long; I was beginning to step back into the edges of my personal life where I was uncomfortable. I tried to accelerate. "We were close when we were younger. Not so much now. She's a dental hygienist. Married a dentist, but not the one she works for. They moved to Vancouver. Two careers, two kids, two cars, two pets. The usual."

"So who died?"

"My wife died of cancer last July."

My words trembled at the fringe of my hearing, as if coming inward to me from a distance, not produced by me.

She lowered her arms from stretching, taking me in. "I'm sorry."

I snapped shut. I had become so skilled at closing off parts of myself to others.

I had to recline casually to disguise my discomfort. Felled by my own statement. Settling into the consolation and support of the mattress, I closed my eyes for a few seconds. To preserve my lie, to escape her squinted studying of me.

Sometimes I was angry at my wife for dying, for causing so much trouble, for causing me so much guilt and pain and confusion. Sometimes, more than anything else, I was angry at her for not trying harder to stay alive. But other times I missed her. So much so that it felt as if only a fraction of each breath was actually making it down into my lungs to sustain me.

Wilma tamed her next few questions. I let out dulled responses in condensed sentences without opening my eyes to look at her. The blackness captured behind my tightened eyelids was infinite, limitless, and I could feel myself drifting off into it like a planet loosed from its orbit.

ᴄᴚᴂ

When I opened my eyes again, it was deeply dark in the room. Silent except for the whirring of air conditioning. From the sourness in my mouth I could tell that I had been asleep for several hours.

When I shifted my position, I found the bedspread folded over me, a pillow mashed beneath my cheek. I was constricted by my clothing tugging at my groin and armpits. For several seconds, I remained stiffly motionless while I reassembled the fragments of how I got there.

I turned carefully, an inch at a time.

She was sleeping on the other half of the bed. But beneath the sheet and blanket. Insulated from me.

Carefully I extracted my arm from beneath the scratchy bedspread and reached out. Tentatively. My fingers met her shoulder, the limp cotton of a T-shirt.

I left them there for longer than I knew I should.

Before I could retract my hand, she lifted the tips of my fingers in her own. Rolled onto her back. Dragged my hand down to her other palm which now lay comfortably waiting between us on top of the bedspread and folded her fingers around mine gently.

"I better go," I insisted softly.

"It's okay," she whispered. "Go back to sleep."

17

The flickering Toronto skyline rolling out before me like a carpet, at midnight, I stand in the unlit living room window of our condo high above the city.

I play a game with myself.

Going very fast.

Always keeping myself focused on where I am going, next week, next month, but never on where I am, here and now in the night.

Friday night comes to me like the quivering pause at the top of a roller coaster, poised for vehement descent. No matter how much I dread it, no matter how much I try to make it otherwise, the weekend is a downward spiral into a pit of loneliness.

My inner voice conspires against me.

Where is Judith? it demands. How long does the night last for her?

Blame flows in rivers.

The voice reminds me that I failed in all my attempts to pry back the oppressive mantle of my wife's depression. Other doctors. Other medication. Pulling with my devotion and patience. Pushing with my disappointment and fear. I could neither deliver her nor reclaim her from a disease that, like an invisible python, was swallowing her whole while she was yet alive, helpless in her own terror.

Out of frustration and guilt, I sought the shallow sanctuaries within my work and career, driving myself to alternate accomplishments.

At the times and places where our lives touched at ever-shrinking junctures, the love I offered her spattered back in my face, like drops of water pinging off hot frying oil. Her untamed responses fuelled by surges of chemicals within her brain that ripped savagely through her emotions and moods. Or by drug side effects that left tigers in her eyes. Repeatedly scalded by the acidic juices of her rage and her rejection and her denunciations, and staggering under the load of trying to carry her along with me as her will to live dissolved. I learned to avoid her to avoid my own pain from her rejection, my own pain from my failure of her. At times, when my fear of facing an uncertain future escaped my grasp, I learned to fear her.

I step back from the wide dark window, the cold glass, the abyss of the eternal November night.

Pushing back from memories that press in on me.

Prowling the rooms like a whiskerless cat, bumping into undetected emotions, I drift to the bedroom.

Without acknowledging the bed, I take a flattened pillow and bunched duvet from where they have been waiting crammed in a closet.

Return to the living room.

Flop onto the couch without undressing, stuffing the pillow under my neck, jerking the duvet around my shoulders like a shield.

The night seems to breathe down on me.

Going fast.

Never where I am.

If you never cease one journey, you do not have to start the next.

18

My sleep diluted by the dawn, I rolled off the edge of the mattress carefully, trying not to disturb her. She came half awake, tucked beneath the sheet on her side of the bed, and tapped my fingers faintly goodbye. I felt for my shoes in the shadows. Flinched at the noise of the door snapping closed as I eased out of her room.

In my matted clothes, I rode the elevator down to my floor amid crisp-suited businessmen on their way to breakfast meetings, walked the corridor to my room nodding politely to fresh-faced tourists, not exactly sure of what I had done nor what our shared night meant, and nurturing distant recollections of coming home from bachelor dates that were, at once, vaguely pleasing and vaguely unsettling.

When I pushed my door open, it scraped across an envelope that had been slipped under the jamb. I caught the envelope in my fingers, closed the door behind me, flicked on lights. I opened the envelope as I walked across the room. Inside were the faxed pages from Michelle. Bless her cheerful heart. I sat heavily in a chair by the window to read them, the blinds pulled open, the pinkish sunrise spilling into the pools of pale yellow lamplight. My eyes felt scratchy. Burned.

I read vigilantly through the five pages, focusing my attention to wring out the significance of each word as I read it, deliberately letting my attention absorb one conspicuous phrase after another. When I finished, I shuffled the pages back into their correct order. Read them again, first to last, without pause.

Then I rattled the pages softly in my fingertips.

Rubbed at my eyes.

Muttered within the deepening flow of my breathing, "All of them..."

I pushed myself up. Stood there. Uncertain.

I looked up to the ceiling. Her? Begin to share again?

I shook my head. No.

I felt chilled.

I stepped to the window. Pressed my hand against the glass, trying to lure the outside heat through into the flattened pads of flesh in my palm and fingertips. Some anomaly between interior air conditioning and exterior humidity caused a mitten of haze to puff up on the glass around my hand.

The five pages told me everything.

I realized it all at once, and all for the first time, like having all of the blood flushed back into my brain. Since my wife's death, I had become so absorbed in engaging the voice I spoke within myself, I had neglected a steady stream of crucial facts and clues coming to me from beyond the screen of my own emotions. I had been purposely whispering into the wind for the comfort of my own words blown back into my face. Buried within the echoing and re-echoing of my guilt and loneliness, I had become detached from my suspicion and my intuition—separated from a potent fusion of doubt and belief that had always been rudimentary to my survival in my business life.

I withdrew my hand from the glass, lifted my elbow, and buffed the hand-shaped condensation with my shirt sleeve. Seeking perception. Clarity.

I stared out above the waking city to the flaring horizon. Trying to see to the ocean. Trying to see across the ocean to the Americas. Then trying to see beyond. To the Bahamas. To the clear constant currents of the Gulf Stream. To places where turquoise waves gently folded into the blinding white sand.

How could that paradise where I had shared my last days with Judith harbour such calumny and deceit?

✧✧

Everything became concentrated in my hotel room, as if I could now only trust things in a place where I could keep constant watch on them, as if they would sheer out of orbit if they drifted out of my vision; I sensed the seeds of a compulsion that anything I let slip out of my direct control would slip out of play.

Boxed in by our open briefcases and notepads, curling pages crowded with inky skeletons of notes and diagrams tossed to the table and bed and floor, separated by cups stained with the dregs of cold coffee, Stanley and I sat across from each other. Looked at each other attentively. Our deductions now worn thin from repetition.

"Okay," Stanley sighed. "You get me out of bed this morning to fly up here from Singapore, jammed in the last open seat in economy class. So we might as well go through it one last time."

I nodded. "As far as it leads."

We pushed our facts along like tired janitors at the end of a long shift pushing the balled dust before them at the end of their brooms.

"Okay," Stanley led off, and continued without waiting for me. "You lean hard on Albert Quan, he caves in and admits that he and the other directors have buckled under to Amsterdam Bank."

"And our financing goes up in smoke."

"And any angle we have to bargain the deal back into play with BSA or Amsterdam is blocked by BSA's threat to blow up the Mayfield Hotel bonds and send me to jail to if you start suing them."

"Then, I find out about Bahamas."

"And, oddly enough, Albert Quan shows up as a director of Global Vest Banking Corporation in the Bahamas."

"Along," I add, "with Kyle Addison from our shop. And Ted Dwyer from the underbelly of Canadian politics. And, even stranger, a big juicy piece of Global Vest is owned by Amsterdam Bank Suisse AG from Geneva."

Like re-chewing food that no longer offered any taste.

"Which," Stanley concluded, digging his elbows into the arms of the chair and shoving his heels out for emphasis, "doesn't make any fucking sense at all."

"Right."

I felt myself proceeding smoothly over this ground, taking ownership of it through our repeated speaking of the facts out loud, converting them from weightless thoughts, swelling them with sound. I could not diminish the impact of the betrayal by denying it. Nor by falsely claiming that I had expected it. Illuminating the shadows revealed what had always been there in the dark. Betrayal had always been an orphaned offspring of the money.

Stanley began redrawing the circle in reverse. "Why would Amsterdam Bank go to all the trouble of threatening Bank of South Asia to force them to weasel out of your bond deal, only to come through the back door and climb into bed with Albert Quan in the Bahamas?"

"And," I added, "what the hell are Kyle Addison and Ted Dwyer doing in the same bed with them?"

I shook my head. Lifted a coffee cup. Empty. Let it clink back into its saucer. Dead end. "Kyle is tearing strips off me eight ways at once on this deal. He wants me dead. For a dead deal. He walks around as if he's never heard of Bank of South Asia. And then he's secretly buddy-buddy with Albert Quan down in the Bahamas."

"Which is the same Bahamas company where Albert Quan is partners with his big nemesis, Amsterdam Bank."

"Meanwhile, back at the ranch in Canada, Kyle and Ted Dwyer are tiptoeing around behind everybody's back to sweet-talk the Senate banking committee so we can be sold out to Atlantic Laurentide."

"So?"

"So what the fuck are they all doing down in the Bahamas in the same company? I don't get it."

"Neither do I," Stanley agreed. "Sit here for three hours and drink enough coffee to put my kidneys on dialysis, neither do I."

I rocked up to my feet, trying to free myself from the ebb in our reasoning. I began to fear that the information on Global Vest was some sort of bait to draw me into a trap. My growing suspicion caused me to pace tentatively, as if there were soft sinkholes lurking in the carpet to trap my advance. "Go down the list of what we've got for possible courses of action. Start with Albert Quan. We could just hand over our documents to the Singapore monetary authorities."

"Which gets you nothing," Stanley replied in monotone, a song we had over-practised. "Maybe, or maybe not, there's enough for them to charge Albert Quan with some infractions. Maybe, or maybe not, he goes to jail. But it still won't get you your financing. And it certainly won't stop Amsterdam Bank from pressuring BSA by threatening to dump their stock. So the remaining directors at BSA will just continue to refuse your financing. Even if they go through the motions of processing a new loan application, you know it won't stand a chance."

"So no difference. Short run or long run."

"Not in your lifetime or mine."

"Next," I listed, "we've got Kyle and Ted Dwyer keeping the home fires burning in Toronto while, in the Bahamas, they go into business with Albert and some Amsterdam Bank subsidiary out of Geneva."

"Which means?"

"I wish I knew."

"And what can you do about it?"

"I wish I knew that as well. I don't know that there's anyone we can report them to, or that there's even anything we can report them for."

"Which leaves us with what?"

"Which leaves us with the ugly truth that, much as I enjoy your company, we sure as shit can't just keep sitting here doing fucking nothing."

"So," Stanley repeated, our arrival at the same finish line, "you've got to get them to show their hand and get some more information."

"Somehow. But not until the sun comes up in Toronto. Another ten or twelve hours."

"Let sleeping dogs lie."

"At least let them sleep."

Our words slipped off the outward edges of our deliberation, leaving an empty table. Gaps. An interval to squeeze out stretches of our spines, calves, bite back on the aftertaste of our coffee.

I sat down and we settled back in fresh silence.

I thought about Stanley losing his job, about him going home to the wife and two sons in the picture on his desk. It suddenly occurred to me that I had deliberately never mentioned my wife's death to anyone outside of the Toronto office; not wanting to sow any suspicion that my abilities were diminished by grief; but, most of all, not wanting to allow polite regrets and condolences to intrude into the space where I sought to escape through hours of working myself to numbness. And Stanley had been too polite to inquire about my personal life in the middle of this crisis. That meant that Stanley still thought my wife was alive. In Stanley's consciousness, I thought strangely, my wife lived and breathed even though Stanley had never met her or known her. Did that mean that I had consigned her to some sort of limbo?

"Amsterdam Bank," Stanley said flatly.

I discarded my thought and chased after Stanley to catch up. "Which leaves Amsterdam Bank," I agreed.

"We know they're involved behind the scenes in Global Vest in some secret deal in the Bahamas."

"Out in the open markets, we know they've gone out and pre-sold Bangkok Commercial's entire bond deal at fire-sale prices. They've contacted our firm in Toronto with some brutal numbers. And we know they've got their clutches into Bangkok Commercial with a bailout offer. All cash. But on cutthroat terms that they're not afraid to put on the table because they know Bangkok Commercial is desperate and they smell blood."

"So what are you going to do about them?"

"I think I've got something worked out with Sanoh Sajjakul. It's based on an interlocking trust structure to hold the bonds."

"Not bad."

"But I need a lot of money."

"How much?" Stanley inquired.

"About ninety million."

"Wonderful."

"Any idea," I wondered aloud, "where we can get it?"

"On what terms?"

"Any terms. You know someone?"

Stanley shrugged. "I might. I can make a call. But how serious are you? Because the terms are not going to be pretty."

"Dead serious."

"This is not going to be some smiling guy from Chase Manhattan."

"Dead serious," I repeated. I flipped his palms loosely. What other choice?

"Okay. You've been warned."

"How soon can you set it up? Today?"

"What's the first Mandarin you ever learned dealing with the Beijing banks?"

"Gaixin shuyou shijian ..."

"That's right. Patience. It takes time."

*

Racing against the fading day.

Sitting at the edge of the bed, a damp towel bunched around my waist, dripping at the back of my neck and elbows from the shower I had left in haste to skid to the ringing telephone, I closed my thrashing conversation on another of Sanoh Sajjakul's returned calls, confirming the details of our patched-together progress, and replaced the receiver tentatively, as if it would burn with another ring as soon as the line was cleared.

Preoccupied, coasting off the impulsive, runaway momentum of our conversation, I stood. I resisted the urge to pace recklessly to the drumming of my thoughts. I began moving away from the bed, keeping my steps short, as if I was seeking to avoid any stumble. Compelled to touch tangible things, running my hand along the crests of the furniture. Of their own accord, my finger-tips sought out hard polished surfaces to tap. I tried to hum a tuneless tune; abandoned it when the repetition became quickly irritating. Drops of water from my wet hair dried on my neck and shoulders. It pushed me, the voice, to seek firmer ground.

I had spent the hours since Stanley had departed on a fleeting handshake pleading out my amendments to our bond contracts with Sanoh Sajjakul.

Telephone calls volleyed back and forth.

As the hours melted.

I had begged up the meeting, pressing my voice into each telephone call when Sanoh Sajjakul hesitated, getting him to flog the bank's attorneys into rushed preparations, cajoling faithlessly when Sanoh Sajjakul balked at inconveniencing the bank's senior directors on scant notice for fear of making them uneasy and uncertain.

Normally, the fervent pace of the money alone would have carried me. I would have regained my equilibrium from it. I would have been lifted by it. Like faster-flowing air under the wings of an aircraft, lifting it out of turbulence.

Now it only delivered raw momentum.

I was, I recognized, negotiating rashly instead of skilfully. No longer intent on success. Only on survival. Only vocalizing as fast as I could, painting my posture big, to save myself from being mauled between the demands of Bangkok Commercial and the intimidation of Amsterdam Bank. Baiting Sanoh Sajjakul and his other bank directors with greed and fear. Sacrificing my margin of profits and principles in equal measure.

Wasting the true potency of the money. Feeding it into a furnace, heating a hothouse, forcing the deal to bloom out of season.

৵৲

Confined within the taxi by the shriek and steamy heat of the streets, I was left without space to escape my fears.

They had no morality, Kyle and Ted Dwyer and Albert Quan who hammered down on me from some fraudulent scheme in the Bahamas. I could feel it, how their actions carried no sense of fairness or of playing by any rules but their own. But, with only this part of their actions revealed, I could not understand the full depth of their motivation. I could only feel the absence of the morality, like feeling the absence of the cable in an elevator car, feeling the floor plummet from beneath your feet, feeling the sickening lurch in the pit of your stomach.

How, I wondered, was I to find my way? How was I to find my own integrity in this void where all morality was temporary, where gusts laden with revenge threatened to blow me off my course?

I shifted in the seat, conscious that I was pushing my feet into the floor for support.

๛๛

Entering Bangkok Commercial Bank's boardroom deep within their office tower, I was immediately grateful to be far removed from the late afternoon's broiling sun and the hot grimy blare of the street that had left me soaked in the armpits and groin of my dark suit at the end of twenty blocks of honking taxi ride. I had enough stacked against me without the heat and humid pollution.

Sanoh Sajjakul was waiting, seated at the boardroom table, flanked by five other men.

He rose, his eyebrows arching in greeting, stepped around to meet me, shook hands with some sly whispered ribbing about one small girl finishing me off for the night; introduced me to the two aging bank directors whom I recalled from previous dealings and to the three younger attorneys who were fresh to me.

In ritual exchange, I collected a palm-full of bilingual business cards.

We sat down to tepid tea in delicate cups and stout contracts in tidy stacks.

The elder directors confirmed their impatience at being hauled on scant notice into an unscheduled meeting by touching fingers on their wristwatches to indicate that they wished to bypass introductory pleasantries. The meeting commenced at once and proceeded without any detour or delay of discussion or debate. It was firmly conducted by Sanoh Sajjakul, and seemed as if it had already been rehearsed many times before I arrived.

The placid interpretation of the contracts by the three youthful attorneys quickly gave way to Sanoh Sajjakul rising, shucking his suit jacket, loosening his tight-tucked shirt from the waistband beneath his sagging stomach to free himself for broader movement, and energetically leading us out into unfamiliar territory. On an oversize pad of flip paper mounted on an easel in one corner of the room, Sanoh Sajjakul, with thick-tipped markers daintily clasped in his puffy fingers, sketched out the deal in bold strokes of brilliant red and green that bled onto the spongy paper in fuzzy lines and lop-sided circles and slanting letters, like out-of-place Christmas lights. Speaking in rapid, clipped English emphasized by stabs and thrusts of his hands, he laid out his matrix of interlocking trusts that connected all of the different assets of the original transferable bonds—thirty-eight separate mortgages on a variety of disconnected housing developments and office complexes and shopping centres in three different cities—to the single group of new non-transferable bonds. Like some strange form of financial polygamy to provide the collateral for the borrowed money from the combined dowries of a harem of wives. One source of new funds servicing all the waiting debts. Yet converting the original transferable bonds into new non-transferable bonds, payable solely to Addison, Beaufort and Shulman, all under the cover of the old bond issue, and all achieved by way of an elaborate alchemy of amendments to the original contracts, so that Bangkok Commercial did not risk any exposure in seeking approval from the central bank for an additional bond offering.

Following Sanoh Sajjakul's discourse, listening as if I were ploughing a path through my own thoughts, registering where the new cash in the diagrams dovetailed with the old contracts on the tabletop, scoring the sinuous nods of assent from around the table, I was relieved that I had not had to launch the scheme on my own in an uphill push against prevailing scepticism.

Bringing his exposition to a peak, Sanoh Sajjakul gave a halting half-bow and concluded with, "So this is how we can restructure everything to defend ourselves against Amsterdam Bank and have Mr. Smith's people provide us with our funds."

An elder director rolled his attention off Sanoh Sajjakul and, without pause, addressed me bluntly. "You are asking us to decline the Amsterdam Bank offer, Mr. Smith?"

Striving for a gesture to collect their confidence, I made my reply precise. "Yes."

"You are asking us to decline eighty-seven million dollars, Mr. Smith?"

"Can you," I reasoned, "afford it at thirteen per cent interest?" I cast the narrow sweep of my eye contact around the table, challenging them, trying to bring all five men along with me. "Can you afford to have a hundred million dollars worth of your corporate paper floating around out there at higher-than-market yield so that it scares everybody who trades it into wondering what's wrong with your credit rating? Before long it becomes a self-fulfilling prophecy and you start getting your notes called in all over the place."

The elderly director paused, gleaning the absence of any dissent in the wavering silence to consolidate his authority and persist. "Will your firm pay us more for our bonds?"

"Yes."

"How much more?"

"I'm not sure exactly. Just yet. But more than Amsterdam Bank wants to pay you."

Sanoh Sajjakul stepped away from the easel and softly settled back in his chair, retracting any tacit support.

On my own now, the wrinkled director and I held each other's attention with exacting voice and unbending gaze in a restrained liturgy of call and response.

"When will you know for us?"

"No matter what we pay you, it will never leak out into the market place because we will be restricted from ever transferring the bonds to any other purchaser."

"There is no benefit to us unless you pay us more. You must."

"We will."

"We know your firm. We know its credit rating from Standard & Poor's. Your firm does not maintain almost a hundred million dollars in treasury reserves or retained earnings."

"No. But we can raise it."

"How?" The senior director rubbed at the liver spots on the back of his hands. Waited determinedly for an answer.

Ritually, they all waited in unison. Their silence drinking up the minutes in the room.

Unsettled in having to pledge so copiously from such negligible foundation, my assertions floating on hope like oil floating on water, I leaned in, steadying myself against the silky grain of the boardroom table with my fingertips. I inhaled for leverage. I dealt it out briskly, summarizing rapidly. "We'll take in your non-transferable bonds. Place them in escrow. Issue our own asset-backed participation notes against the bond collateral and bond income. We'll only need your bonds to carry enough interest to meet the market. Your cost of funds will be much closer to market rates. Certainly much lower than what Amsterdam Bank is holding you ransom for."

I nudged the attorneys with a quick flick of my eyes and concentration. The three attorneys nodded. It was possible.

Assured that the quota of protection to his position by the bank's attorneys was adequate, the senior director asked me. "Do you have a new agreement to guarantee that to us?"

"It's all in the amendments before you."

"Why should we accept those amendments when you are going to default on your first agreement?"

"Because I promise you."

The director quit me. Clicking his partial plate behind his pale lips. Irresolute.

Aware that I had been tripped into the error of accelerating prematurely to a covenant predicated on my own credibility, which had been rendered both insufficient and suspect in their eyes by the events of the last week, I had to smother my words behind a poorly executed hand gesture of opening my palm to the contracts to indicate that they confirmed my commitment.

The director waited me out, wielding the stillness. He canvassed the table with a frown of inquiry.

With the degree of their deliberation measured out in their further waiting, the others turned the decision back to the senior director, who demanded, "How long will it take you to raise the funds?"

The words were brittle around their edges.

The directors would not be persuaded with my vacant promises. "We can begin raising the funds immediately," I stated. "We only need you to sign the amendments to your bond contracts to give us non-transferable bonds and drive Amsterdam Bank out of the picture."

"On that alone you will have the funds for us?"

"Yes."

"There will be no further problems?"

"We will have your funds for you."

The director swallowed off the last of his cold tea with a grimace, shrugged. "When?"

I snapped my palm face down. "Give me forty-eight hours."

"In forty-nine hours we will sign with Amsterdam Bank."

"Forty-eight is all I need."

"Forty-eight, Mr. Smith, is all you have."

Ink.

Handshakes around the table. Parting pledges in my grip.

Pissing away promises I prayed to keep.

What you went through for the money.

19

In the fiery residue of the afternoon, I returned to the hotel. Stanley was waiting for me in the lobby bar, leaning back in a low armchair from a tall glass brimming with ice cubes, beckoning me with rolling fingers, slackened in expression and posture.

I took it as a good sign that he had not left Bangkok, and veered across the lobby to where he sat. I was reminded of the weight of the signed contracts in my briefcase as I settled it to the floor and my wrist was relieved of the burden. Beginning to tally up that, and other, improvements in my situation and spirit, I dropped into the opposite armchair.

Stanley set his glass on the lacquered coffee table at our knees, interrupting my cursory assessment. "I've got something for you."

I scrubbed my palm into my sweaty forehead. "What?"

"Benjamin Lim."

"Who is?"

"Your money."

I frowned. "One guy? A hundred million?"

"China Success Leasing," Stanley declared.

I stalled, puzzled.

Stanley continued rapid fire. "Albert Quan has been pulling

those Mayfield Hotel bonds like a knife. Slashing every deal I brought to the bank for the past year, as well as my career. Because I let China Success have an option clause in their contract that let them walk away from the Mayfield deal without any penalty when the real estate market melted down last year."

"I still don't get it."

"How do you think I got the Mayfield Hotel deal from China Success Leasing in the first place?"

I waited.

"Benjamin Lim," Stanley announced. "He's chairman."

I nodded appreciatively. "I didn't know your contacts went to the top of the blue chips on the Hong Kong exchange."

"He and my father went to school together, started as junior managers with Heng Seng Bank. They stayed close all their lives. After my father died, he gave my youngest sister away at her wedding last year."

I leaned back, opened my palms. Impressed.

Stanley affirmed, "Uncle Benny."

"Indeed."

"I finally got tired of being stopped out of every option by Bank of South Asia because I took it on the chin for Benny and China Success when the real estate market crashed. So I called him. Took a couple of calls to track him down, but I got through to him on his private cell phone number."

"You called in your favour."

Stanley shrugged. "You know Asian business. You never say anything directly. You call on some other matter and you talk around the favour without mentioning it."

"And it worked."

"It worked."

The money, the fealty it demanded. Everything sudden. Change always blowing from all sides. Bringing risk with every opportunity, and opportunity with every risk. You could never see your course over the horizon; your planning always had to include a measure of hope. But never take your sails out of the wind or the money would abandon you in its wake.

Stanley continued. "We can fly up to Hong Kong tonight and meet him for breakfast tomorrow morning. Or we can meet him for early lunch when he flies down here to Bangkok tomorrow. But then we'll have less time because he'll be running out the door to make his tee-off time. He's booked to play golf all afternoon with some big shooters in the steel and chemical industry."

"Let's wait until lunch."

"You sure?"

"I need tonight."

"What for?"

"Let me call my office when Toronto opens. See if I can smoke out anything on this Nassau thing."

"Sure."

Our next step agreed, we settled back into our armchairs on our decision.

"You make out okay at Bangkok Commercial?" Stanley inquired.

"Yeah. Good." I lifted my briefcase an inch, let it thud down on the carpet, proof and promise in its sturdy drop.

Stanley lifted his drink to pull a final swallow off the lip of the glass, shifted to rise.

There was reprieve to be appreciated within the briefness of this breath.

There was also, I sensed, more for me to say.

Like stepping around a blind corner with my opening words.

"Stanley," I asked, "what do you get out of this?"

Stanley shrugged. Obvious. "The satisfaction of seeing Albert

Quan not get what he wants. And Benny Lim will take care of me. You know business in this part of the world. Layered like an onion with families and favours. It couldn't work otherwise."

The rest came to me so naturally, so distinctly, that I could not imagine there being anything else to say at that time, at that place, in my life.

"Would you be interested in starting a new firm with me?"

Stanley hesitated.

"Our own firm. Partners. We'll spin enough cash out of this to incorporate, rent and staff two offices. You handle this side of the world, I'll handle the other side."

Stanley hid behind a frown. Deliberating. "Possibly."

I waited him out, let his bubble of doubt rise to the surface.

"How much slack is in the deal?"

"We flip the bonds back to Amsterdam. Your half has to be twice what BSA is offering you in severance. Without Albert Quan's lying fucking fingers wrapped around your throat when you get out of bed every morning."

"My other job offers?"

"You going to go to work on salary in Beijing and get buried in some department at Bank of China?"

"What's in the future after this deal?"

I reached out into the empty air for something to close with. "You get to be Uncle Stanley to my kids."

"Let me think about it."

Business in this part of the world layered like an onion.

৶৹৵

It blew through every minute now.

The urge to run.

Like a stone stuck in my shoe. Tread carefully, in check, and it didn't bother me. Come down hastily or rashly, as I had been doing all afternoon, and suffer little bites of panic.

Alone in my room, trying to hide behind the safety of the locked door, I flopped on the bed, wedged my hands under the weight of my thighs to still the tremor in my fingertips.

Why not just walk away?

Let Kyle choke on it.

Let Kyle and Ted Dwyer dance themselves to death.

I'd had more than enough. For more than long enough.

Bad enough Amsterdam Bank throwing its weight around in Singapore, bullying Bank of South Asia. But that I could at least dismiss as the vagaries, and the cruel undercurrent, of the business we practised with the money.

Never any support from Kyle any more. That tasted of heartburn and betrayal.

Nothing but criticism and threats. Nothing but arguments any more. Pulling the rug out from under me in cold disregard every chance he got. As if he had made it his mission to chastise me for letting my personal life interfere with my career this last year. As if I had grossly breached some unpublished rule, left the firm vulnerable, in suffering personal loss. As if, in letting my concentration leak, I had insulted him personally; gored his shining pride in me.

Why stay? Why even bother?

Always, the urge to run lured me backward to the rhetorical question of what was I to do those mornings she couldn't drag herself to work, those mornings she begged me to stay with her. The urge and the question inseparable. Those mornings when I tried mightily to prove that I could do both, succeed in my career and care in my personal life. Stretching myself paper thin and still failing to cover all the frayed edges of her needs, the company's needs, my needs.

The mornings I stayed home with her, Kyle steered the deals away from me.

The mornings I left her and went to the office, I suffered my failing of her in her dark, empty eyes, in doors closing behind me.

Either way, my sense of myself was diminished.

It left me feeling constantly vulnerable; and I knew of no other way to compensate except to push myself harder.

Now, as I saw it from this distant side of the world, I held only who I was in this deal. If I failed, I would have to leave too much of my past, leave too many parts of myself, behind, and I would never regain sufficient forward momentum to cross over to a fresh life. If I quit, ran, tried to start over in something else, somewhere else, I would always carry defeat in my luggage, never able to discard it, never knowing when it would undermine me again.

If I did not stick with this, stick it out, I would cease being who I was.

သာ

I stepped from the elevator into the fragrance of a thousand blossoms.

Like heaps of jewels, shimmering tropical flowers spilled from massive ceramic bowls on the marble floor and pedestals ringing the entrance of the hotel's penthouse restaurant.

The backs of my hands were still pink from showering, where no amount of steaming water could alleviate the tension. I had spent my final minutes staring into the precision of the full-length mirror on the bathroom door, computing the depth and distance remaining in my sprint to regain control of my life. As much as I wanted to elude being branded with failure, I wanted also to emerge from my shadows. I was confident of my resolve for my career; if I could maintain my energy and focus and luck, I could re-weave the money into a successful deal and prevail over those betraying me.

But, when I let my concentration fall off the horizon, distant by days, of success for my bond deal, the voice overtook me with misgivings closer to the evening.

How did I reach out again to anyone? In convincing myself that my retreat inward was minimal and temporary, had I left myself more incompetent of caring than I realized? Face down in a few inches of water you drowned the same as sinking in bottomless ocean. What if I had left myself with so little emotional substance to offer that no one would want me?

The disorder of those thoughts lingered in some part of each breath. I had never felt more alone, unsure. Not since the emptiness of my first night alone after Judith's death. Since then, I had spent everything in trying to keep that hollowness from trickling into my days.

I began checking the tables to see if she had yet arrived, and found myself resenting other diners embarking on the chosen pleasures of their evening seemingly unencumbered by worry or uncertainty.

An oasis of starched white table clothes. Crystal. Broad windows. On the other side of the glass, in the residual blue shadows of dusk, the thick humid air and oily pollution of Bangkok was disguised as a vast palace of rippling and flowing lights. At the horizon, a ragged orange-and-grey sunset was breaking into fragments through the low, murky sky. The colours evoked some sudden and vital memory of college summer vacation latitudes. Inside my head I could detect the smell of dusty, newly mown grass carrying the tranquillity of idle afternoons, a carpet to evenings of vagrant hearts, careless love. As I attempted to focus on the memory, seeking to bring its solace into myself, her voice interrupted me and it was almost painful for me to lose it.

"Hello."

I turned.

She glided off the elevator. A sleeveless top, flowery skirt. Fresh-scrubbed.

It confused me to see her so cheerfully restored from her dog-tired collapse in her room, overwhelmed by her work and papers.

As I took a step towards her, a persistent eddy of doubt washed over me. How needy I must seem to her, dozing off on her bed, snoring probably.

"Very nice of you to invite me," she announced merrily.

I was forced to recognize that, despite my inclination when insulated by a telephone call where we did not have to make any eye contact, my invitation may have been more a consequence of contrition than desire.

"Well... thank you... for last night." Neutrally, I tried to grin; it came out chancy, indistinct.

It left her only able to comment, "You're welcome."

Was there, I began to wonder, a husband or live-in boyfriend, waiting for her at home? Someone she would be spending this weekend with if she were there, making pasta, wine by candle-light, reading the Sunday paper in bed over croissants and cof-fee? Was I missing some clue in her voice and diction?

I indicated the maître d' hovering with menus in hand. "You ready?"

She nodded explicitly, but said nothing further.

The maître d' led us to our table.

I walked beside her without speaking.

Seated, I tried to ease us into it quickly, tried to improve her impression of me and cancel her image of me flopped on her bed, by jesting immediately with some lame punch line to ordering drinks. She ordered white wine, sat almost primly compared to the previous evening's casual ease. I requested Scotch more out of habit than craving.

She said, "Lovely view."

"Yes." I became aware of my lack of fluency with the experience. Being at a table, waiting for drinks with a woman other than Judith. I had not done this with another woman, even for business meetings, in my months alone. My intent felt ambiguous, my intuition seemed absent.

She took up the wine glass as soon as it arrived and gulped off an ample swallow, offered a flimsy smile of apology.

I cautiously lifted my own glass rather than risk acknowledging that I had watched, not wanting her to be embarrassed into thinking she had to explain, not wanting to draw attention to my ungainly steps to pick up from where we had shared our sleeping.

Politely, I asked, "How'd your presentation go today at the conference?"

She brightened. "Really well. We were supposed to have an hour for questions afterwards. We went for two hours."

"Congratulations." I traced gentle circles on the starched tablecloth with my fingers, our impersonal topics of conversation prematurely depleted.

"My apologies," I offered, "for passing out on you last night. Hogging half your bed."

She shrugged.

"Hope I didn't keep you from getting some rest."

She tried to disguise it with indulgence. "Not the first time."

(And would that be about the plane, or at home? Best not to open it.)

I nodded in mute penance, giving it wide berth.

Severely, I was reminded how I had let my wife slip away in such prudence and restraint. Avoiding questions when I did not want to deal with the answers. Avoiding her when I sensed she was ripe to unleash her anguish and rage. Keeping my distance in the shadows cast by her despair at times when she had exhausted my energy for dealing with her.

Coming back in from my thoughts, I made an effort to focus on Wilma's face and words. My lack of attention, I saw, had broadened her fidgeting frown and set her fingers jiggling; she had let her gaze dip to the table top where she picked absently at some unseen stain with her fingernail. I promptly regretted my lapse, and felt petty in my inability to award equal value to her circumstances.

Disappointed in myself for not knowing how to compensate her, I lifted the Scotch, intending to eclipse my discomfort with a robust swallow, but limited myself as soon as the smoky, burning taste spread under my tongue and caused a spasm in my empty stomach.

She matched me, raising her wine delicately and restricting herself to a long, slender sip.

On the table, I methodically rotated my glass with my fingers.

When she stopped drinking we sat in silence except for the grinding of my glass against the tablecloth.

I fell back against remnants of mislaid empathy.

"Sorry if I seem a little distant," I told her. "I really did want to call you for this." Then I felt compelled to clarify that I had not brought to the table any expectations of her to repeat last night's ministrations. "To thank you for last night. For listening. For the Tylenol. For letting me sleep."

"You're welcome. It was a nice invitation."

"And I wanted to see you again."

"I wanted to come." She wrapped her reply in a tempered consent that made obvious my responsibility to carry our conversation to a less guarded level. She looked at me. Watching.

My patience had been bled thin by deceit wafting from the Bahamas and by having to lean so deeply into the hollowness of my promises to the bank directors. I was blunt. "Are you married?"

She bounced my inquiry back at me flatly. "Don't I seem it?"

"You don't act it"

"Do you?"

"I told you," I stated.

"And did your wife die from cancer?"

"I told you."

She balked, her self-consciousness bunching in wrinkles across her nose. It was like having a mirror mounted across from my face, reflecting my own sudden unease.

"But," she continued firmly, "you don't sound like your wife died from cancer."

"How can you say that?"

"Because she didn't. Did she?"

Instinctively, I hesitated, appraised her reticently; she had provoked within me a shivering current of anger and ambiguity. Gathering the threads of my reply, I tested my denials; discarded them when they were wanting. Finally, I admitted, "No."

"No," she repeated. At least allowing me to continue by not rising to accusation or reproach.

"She committed suicide. Last summer." I shed the words as I pronounced them, wanting to leave them behind us, but conscious that they now became pieces of my life left in hers. Then waited without further explanation for her reaction, assessing her.

She avoided my scrutiny, snapped up her wine glass, and drank off the remaining wine in three quick, vicious swallows.

"I'm sorry," she said, placing the stemmed glass back onto the table. "Truly."

"Thank you." I shrugged off her condolence. Ducking her overture. I could not help thinking of times in the weeks before my wife's death. When I would come home to find her sitting motionless with a bloodless face in front of the television set, the television not on, starring into the tunnel of an empty screen. My response then also dulled, and inadequate to bury a problem I no longer knew how to solve.

When I re-firmed my gaze across the table, I found Wilma blinking; unsure, now that we had come to the end of it, if she had gone too far, lost me.

"How could you be so sure?" I asked.

"Like AIDS, most cancers are long deaths," she explained. "Surviving spouses are changed forever, watching someone they love waste away. They experience almost as much pain as the dying spouse. They usually try to learn as much as they can about the cancer to compensate for their helplessness during the treatments and hospital visits. And they usually can't help themselves from being a lot more specific about some of the details when they explain it to someone else."

"And I didn't talk about anything."

"You didn't talk about the truth."

"I only seem to be able to talk about it inside myself. Some things are too hard for me to listen to out loud."

"Did she react to some type of trauma? Was she diagnosed with any type of depression?"

"Depression. She was diagnosed uni-polar. Was being treated. But she hated the medication. Said the side effects were worse than the depression. We had her hospitalized twice in the last year, but she would leave as soon as her medication was stabilized after a few days. She hid everything. In the end, she just went deeper and deeper inside herself. And never came up."

"I am sorry."

Disgraced and defensive from being found out, I dropped the question of her marriage.

We coasted down into dinner as if mutually conceding it was better to be there than not. Service was slow. Conversation was sporadic: a run at her research; and then, in a scurry of aborted remarks, a bag of business travel anecdotes. I was grateful she did not return to my deceit. We never finished our plates, but we drained the final pouring from a bottle of Chardonnay.

I found the chilled white wine tasted somehow familiar and reassuring in its incidental excess. It was something plentiful when everything else seemed a scarcity.

"Thank you," she said as she sipped off the last of the glass. "For dinner."

I allowed myself to let go of enough of my tension and uncertainty to notice her eyes, wet with alcohol, restless in the quick flickers of pale dining room light, the smoothness of her eyelids somehow threatened by the keen fringe of her razored hair whenever she twisted her head.

I nodded wordlessly in reply, mitigating the obligation.

"You haven't told me what you're working on here," she reminded me. "Your meetings in Singapore and Bangkok."

"I'm working on a bond deal."

"Is it interesting?"

"Sometimes."

"Is it big?"

"I suppose."

"How much?"

"A hundred million." Instantly, I tried to drink off the magnitude so it did not appear a boast or an exhibit.

She wiped delicate creases of perplexity from her brow with her fingertips.

"What's it like?" she asked.

"What?"

"That much money."

"Like it's too much."

She stared at me adamantly, persuading me of her refusal to accept my attempt to evade speaking of what worried me most.

Slowly, she shook her head, a fresh chance. "No."

"What?"

"Not how much. The work. What's it like for you to do it? What's it like for you to do whatever it is you do with that much money?"

My hesitation and reticence was a stubborn reflex. I had learned to prosper at the elbows of authority by closing the discussion at an initial question about the general nature of a deal, at a point where my actions could be comfortably substantiated by fact, before I could be pursued into the deeper workings of the negotiations, where progress hinged upon instinct and guesswork, and I often had no proof to support my actions. Wanting to be genuine for her, I was frustrated by not being able to surface easily. Under her eye, I recalculated my candour against the wine in my hand.

She would not cease waiting.

"Do you really want to know about that?" I asked. "Do you really want me to bore you by talking shop over dinner?"

"I want to know about you."

"Why?"

"I've already told you enough about me."

I trusted my measure of how far away she existed; almost anonymous; not close enough to be a threat. I said, "It makes you lose touch with reality sometimes."

"How does that affect your life?"

"Spills back on you sometimes. Like heartburn."

"Then why do you do it?"

"I don't know." I shrugged, wanting to steer clear of my troubled doubt, hide behind swift denial.

"You must have some reason."

"It's how I put one foot ahead of the other."

"Is that all you have," she asked, "putting one foot in front of the other?"

"In the beginning it was what I did."

"Now?"

"It's gone from what I do, to who I am."

"And what's that?"

"Same as for you."

She waited, questioning.

"Do you," I explained, "ever think of yourself as anything other than a doctor?"

She did not answer, waited for more.

I added, "What else do you want it to be? The meaning of life?"

"What about fulfilment," she stressed. "And hope for a better future. Don't you have any of that?"

"I suppose so," I admitted. I glanced down to the table, jiggling my glass, stalling to complete my reply. "I just suppose I've forgotten where I put most of it these days."

"Did you have it when you wife was alive?"

"When the depression wasn't there, nothing was easier than being together. Planning our future."

She wet her lips. She raised a finger.

I sensed she did not need to pause to absorb my words. I sensed she was withholding her response. I realized, when I did not claim title to it, I had let something unspoken come between us.

She tipped her glass steeply, drained the last trace of wine.

I watched her breasts bounce as her diaphragm jumped with a hiccup.

She bit back on it. "Why did you ask me to dinner?"

Like collecting a toll for her presence.

I came to a standstill rather than confess my gratitude for her kindness and caring; afraid to paint myself as an emotional indigent; more afraid that any mention of our mutual isolation could be construed as salacious pursuit. (Here we are…two lonely people in an exotic city…safe from prying eyes…)

She intruded into my empty pretence. "How much longer are you going to keep doing it?"

"Doing what?"

"How much longer are you going to just keep tearing around out there? Thinking you're escaping."

"Escaping what?"

"Your wife's suicide."

I smothered my response. This is not the conversation I had expected to have with her. Not this.

"Lying to yourself that you're all right. Always working nonstop. And always have the guilt and the hurt catch up with you when you least expect it. You keep pushing harder and faster to escape it. And eventually it drops you with a heart attack."

I was afraid to reply. How could I tell her that the pain had become its own living thing within me? Separate, yet a part of me at the same time. Like a white light growing brighter while I remain dimmed.

"You do that," she said, "don't you?"

I wanted to pin her beneath my rebuttal, austere and coldly lethal, but worried that my words would wound her deeper tissues. And I feared the unknown nature of her reproach.

Not to lie, I confessed to something different. "It's better than what I used to do."

"And what was that?"

"For months, I used to look for her on the street. While I was driving or riding in cabs. I'd try to make her appear. And she wouldn't. And then when I least expected it, when it had been weeks and I was on the verge of giving up, it would be her at some street corner. Hair. Eyes. So close it was her sister. And it would fucking stop my heart."

"But it wasn't her."

"Wouldn't matter. My eye would zero in on her. I'd want to see who she was, where she was going. What she was thinking and feeling. I would try to piece together that one thing that had hurt her so badly she had never told anyone about it. And I would try to push my love through the glass to reach that secret hurt within her so she wouldn't hurt any more. And it would make Judith come back for a minute. And then, always, when she disappeared in the rearview mirror after I passed her, it would be like losing her all over again. Like digging a fresh hole."

Recklessly, I swigged off my wine, raised my fingers for the check.

She mouthed a profanity, rocked her head gloomily, could not mask how she clenched her jaw around the tail of the word.

Something about it made me afraid of how far I had gone.

I signed the check, pushed back my chair, stood without comment.

She came with me as if appeased by my asperity and abrupt conclusion.

Aided by jet lag and fatigue, a mild inebriation tugged at me as I moved with her out of the dining room. Lightness ballooned in my head, heat crept up my face. I concentrated on placing my steps in tempo with hers.

Spiralling down into silence, we walked together to her room. We halted as we reach her door.

She turned from me, opened her purse, and hunted out her key.

I touched her shoulder. It seemed fair. She touched mine on the plane.

She stiffened with precaution, turned back to me.

She checked the perimeter of the hallway, as if some obscure sanction hovered there. Wrung out a frown of dubious intent.

It progressed like feeling out vaguely recollected dance steps.

"I've got piles of work," she said.

"So do I. I've got an urgent phone call that I've got to make back to Toronto on this deal."

"And I'll have to get at it soon."

"Me too."

I tried to make her hesitation and second thoughts my own to protect myself against the faintest prick of her rejection. By going away from her, I could ensure that she did not go away from me. In the disquiet of her face and hands, I could sense she was rushing to do likewise.

I backed away from her a pace. The distance allowed our eyes to meet.

She hesitated some evident seconds, looked away from me, then drew the plastic key-card from her purse, slid it into the lock, pushed the door inward. She followed the swinging door into the room, stood holding it, twisted back. "It's been a while since anybody looked at me like that."

"Like what?"

"Like you wanted to take me to the senior prom. Thank you."

She waited, avoiding my eyes.

I moved to her in the doorway, trying to clear the soft smears of alcohol from my vision.

She held the door open with her shoulders, leaning back.

I stayed inches away from her.

The door began to push her into me.

I shuffled. Kissed her.

(Did I know how to do this any more?)

She kissed back.

Feeling her reciprocate my desire, I warmed with the first unforced happiness in a branch of my memory that seemed to flow forward only from the day of Judith's death and seemed to contain only a record of days marked by loss. It made me feel capable, for the first time, of resisting the voice prying between my thoughts. As if sensing the thaw in my emotions, the voice stiffened its reprimand: only bitter mistrust and intense focus on the money to the avoidance of all mental and emotional distraction will rescue me from failure ordained out of the Bahamas. This will be my undoing.

She let the kiss run out, but averted another by pulling me in and slipping her face past my cheek.

I held her awkwardly. In my hand on her back, I could feel her heart beating as if I was touching it. I abandoned my attempts to say any more, and was content to ignore the voice in experiencing the physical closeness to her, encountering her breathing against me and feeling the warmth and moistness of her breath against my cheek and throat.

In our clumsy actions, I could sense unspoken thoughts.

She said, "We can't just keep standing here."

She sagged, feeling at my fingertips as if she was filling with sand. She began to pull away from me, churning against the door with her hips.

I felt as if I had used up all my words for her, as if my desire had lain buried too deep, and I now lacked sufficient substance to take us further.

We needed, both of us, time to go slowly, time to be present with each other.

The money will not spare this to me.

The money, the urgency of it like a lethal undertow, dragged me against my will. Stranded on a shoal of deceit, my bonds demanded rescue. The money would, I knew from harsh experience, magnify the least postponement, the least flicker of doubt, the least delay of judgment or action. Everything with the money was leveraged on a brutal fulcrum. It could inflate my delay of a hundred minutes with her into a loss of a hundred million dollars; several hours with her costing the wages of several thousand people for a lifetime.

I let my arms drop from her.

I must first deal with other things.

I was separated from Toronto by a twelve-hour time difference; it will be midnight there during my meetings tomorrow. If I did not connect with Kyle now, I would have nothing for my approaching morning, nothing to stand on during my negotiations tomorrow with Stanley and Benjamin Lim.

I stepped back.

She made no attempt to stop me.

I withdrew into the hall.

She scarcely nodded, shrugged out her acknowledgment, trying to let me know that she understood even though it was obvious that she did not want to.

It seemed to me I had been taking far too much from her, taking last night, taking at dinner. The feeling intruded, fully formed, into the moment—perhaps some sense, oddly imported into my caring about her, from my ingrained instinct for balance in business negotiations. I deeply wanted to give something back to her, even if it was nothing more than space, quiet. I hoped it would be enough.

I found myself hoping that she has been truthful in implying that her career was as cruel a mistress as mine; so that she will be able to touch a similar place of vehement disappointment within herself; so that she will know what I feel and be consoled by the knowledge that I am not dropping her with impunity.

In acquiescing to the intransigent demands of the money, I have left her no choice.

She rolled off the door to let it close, squeezing herself out of my view.

Until I was alone.

Sad in my acceptance of it.

Nothing more to be said about it.

↭

I got Kyle at home, interrupting his Sunday morning leisure.

"Not a hell of a lot in your emails yesterday, Paris. You got anything cooking out there or not?"

"It's coming."

"Well it better start coming a hell of a lot faster. We can't give you any more time. Ted's had more meetings with Atlantic Laurentide. And with the Senate banking committee. This thing has got to be fixed now. And, for your amusement-and-or-edification, let me be sure to emphasize the part about right-this-fuckin'-minute."

"Kyle, what happened to March tenth? Coming soon, I know. But we've still got a little bit of time here."

"No we don't!"

"I don't see what's changed."

"Because I say it has."

"Wonderful."

"And that's exactly the smart-ass attitude that got us into this whole mess, Paris. That's exactly why I have absolutely no faith in you."

"Look, I've been locked in meetings with Bangkok Commercial. We've got some new goal posts."

"What's it going to get us?"

"Kyle, you know that Bank of South Asia screwed us because Amsterdam Bank leaned all over them."

"All water under the bridge now. And it won't make any difference to our capital requirements when we've got to pay out a shit-load of money we don't have."

"By the way, Kyle. Did you ever know Albert Quan? From the old days perhaps. He claims he's a Yale man."

"Never met him. Never heard of him. Don't know him. And I wouldn't be too sure about that Yale stuff."

"Why?"

"I don't have to tell you about Asian business, Paris. Status conscious to the point of death. First thing they do when they start to make some money is give a big endowment to a big-name university. Then run home with an honorary degree and paste it up on their wall to impress everybody."

"Well, give me another few days."

"I can't see what difference it's going to make."

"Just hold a few days."

"I don't think so, Paris. I think you're sunk. And I think you've sunk us. Have I made that clear?"

"Yes."

"Absolutely clear?"

"Fine."

"So don't come sucking up when you get home and ask us to

re-cut the deal. And don't ever fucking say within my earshot that I didn't warn you."

"Fine."

I hung up, feeling as if I was letting go of a tow rope. As thankful for my liberty from the stinging admonition as I was fearful to be adrift in menacing currents.

Kyle was lying in his denial of Albert Quan; and lying further, in his inflated irritation and impatience, about something else. Except I did not know what. Or how much. Like dropping a pebble into an inky well and now having to wait for the distant splash; not knowing how long to wait or even if there will be water at all at the bottom.

I realized I was being deceived. Betrayed. I hungered for reprisal, yet I knew from instinct and experience that I must restrain myself from irate response until I was more fully armed with the outcome of tomorrow's meeting with Stanley and Benjamin Lim.

But my emotions, like the events of this night, were tangled. I was impatient for victory. It grumbled in my brain in spaces made empty by the wine.

Questions gnawed within me at ripening wounds unprotected by any answers.

How did I avoid succumbing to Kyle and his partners? Ending up outcast and broke. Maybe for life. I had seen it: men destroyed by hostile takeovers gutting their firms, or castigated in the headlines by charges layered with rumours, their integrity watered down, like weak tea, to polite disregard. Rendered impotent by descent into alcohol and tranquillizers. Banished from the game.

How did I avoid rolling over and joining Kyle and his conspirators out of fear of failure? I could leverage what I knew against Kyle by revealing it to him; then keep my mouth shut. Kyle would keep me close to maintain my silence. I would only have to wait a few years for him to retire, leaving me with the keys to the cash box and knowing where all of the bodies were buried.

I was determined not to be defeated by their collusion and deceit.

I was equally determined that it not cost me my understanding and compassion and integrity. I knew without the least breath of doubt that, in choosing a plot to crush them in sweet vengeance, I would be choosing the road they travelled. In striking back in the same manner, devoid of truth, savouring the suffering of my enemies, I would be adopting an ethic of victory at any cost—with the real cost being to myself; eventually becoming incapable of suffering any slight without reprisal; becoming, inch by vengeful inch, a liar, a cheat, and a betrayer.

Calling it business.

Measuring my success in dollars.

Beneath the swift current of the questions, the voice lurked in darker thoughts like a shadowy eel. It insinuated that less energy pumped into my career would have left me with more energy to sustain Judith. It beckoned me back into the snare that I must validate my choice of committing to my career at the cost of my marriage.

Still seated on the edge of the bed from the telephone call, I flopped back hard, arms and shoulders slack.

How did I build something out of this rather than just let them tear me down?

How did I make my own life out of all of this?

I closed my eyes, tried to see though my circumstances to the other side, tried to locate a path that would lead me to where it will be peaceful again.

Was this my last best chance?

I limped to the bathroom, trying to dissipate my agitation by moving away from the telephone. I urinated in an impatient arc, trying to locate in the echo off the wall tiles some distraction from the doubt filling my mind in the wake of the testy telephone call.

At the sink, I splashed water onto my face urgently. Blotted if off with a towel laying damp from my shower, assessing my reflection in the mirror.

Who am I any more?

The stress showed in white creases at the corners of my mouth. The lack of sleep showed in vulpine darkness under my eyes. This portrait of deficits distressed me.

I pulled back from the mirror.

I was, I warned the voice, better than this.

I worked to silence the voice, which continued to resonate with spite and acrimony at Kyle's deceit, trying to concentrate instead on my meetings today with Sanoh Sajjakul. I could feel threads of momentum beginning to twine together. Not the old breakneck adrenaline. But something more. Something from being back in the game with Sanoh Sajjakul. Something that also rose out of the disjointed progression of my dinner with Wilma. More a sense of possibilities that expanded like deep breaths.

If I did not keep moving forward with these beginnings, I risked being swept backwards by the current rushing against me.

I wanted more.

20

The first time I sleep with her something unusual happens. We come together in a suite on the top floor of an expensive downtown hotel after a glittering downtown party.

"I've never done this before," she tells me.

"Neither have I," I say.

"Never anything like this. I just met you a couple of hours ago."

I know that, in shaving our confessions down to a measure of time while omitting mention of the excitement of letting our raw attraction race unchecked, our lies are only partial, at least no worse than the ones played to get through a day. That we both let them pass without a word or a glance is, I sense, something truthful; not some synthetic virginity of a one-night pick-up, but more our shared desire not to crowd our moment by any past populated with other relationships.

Our omissions lead us into each other's arms in urgency, and an excess that drowns out any doubt.

It is not until later that it is not usual.

I think about it constantly each of the next days at the office and alone at home. I find myself asking if my confusion is the result of refusing to join those men I drank Scotch with, who always pronounce that the world is full of broken-hearted and *easy women. Or whether it is a result of refusing to allow my private suspicions, which always insinuate that I am too easy and the world is full of women who will break my foolish heart. I am afraid my confusion will be obvious to her if I see her again, and she will misinterpret it as ambivalence, causing her to discard me in cold fury. So I do not call her.*

And the unusual thing?

The unusual thing is that I wake in the middle of the night and, instead of being asleep beside me, she is crying softly to herself.

I feel instantly concerned for her, as if everything inside me has turned over roughly.

Yet, immediately, simultaneously, I sense the liability of the situation into which I am waking. I keep my eyes pressed closed and do not move, fearful that catching her in her private distress might cause her humiliation that she will carry out of the darkness into the approaching morning.

I listen.

Her crying is a progression of muffled sniffing and swallowing.

Isolated in feigned sleep, I search my actions and intent for some degree of fault. Has something happened after she has so freely agreed to stay?

No further ahead, I roll onto my side to face her across a furrow of darkness.

"What's wrong?"

She twitches, startled by my voice.

"You okay?" I ask.

"Sorry," she sighs. "Sorry-sorry-sorry. Sorry I woke you."

"It's all right."

"I kept telling myself to go into the bathroom, but I'm just too damn exhausted to move. What time is it?"

I twist to the luminous face of the bedside clock radio. "It's five after four."

We had stopped an hour ago; like falling off a cliff. My eyes burn from lack of sleep. I stretch, sore with fatigue.

"I can get up now and go home," she suggests. "You can stay, get some more sleep."

Is it best that we cannot see each other; her distress, my worry that I was part of it?

"Do you want to talk about why you're crying?"

"No."

"Was it because you came here with me?"

"No."

"Should we have not done this?"

"No."

I try to visualize an expression for her face which will convince me that her denials, so methodical and determined, are not merely to preserve her privacy. "Don't just get up and go home," I tell her.

"Why not?"

"I care about you. I care about you crying."

"It's not important. Sorry."

"Why don't you tell me about it?"

"Why?"

"Maybe just because I've offered to listen."

I feel her shift, hear her scrubbing her fingers against her face.

"I woke up and started thinking that I broke off an engagement a month ago. And now this is what my life's become. In bed with…"

"Me."

"No. Not like that. About all the time I loved him for two years, and I never wanted him as much as I wanted you tonight after only knowing you for a few hours."

"I didn't know you were engaged."

"You couldn't have."

I wait, not knowing if there will be more.

"Our engagement just slowed down to nothing because of me. We just thought it would be better to wait and see."

I do not know how to respond. There is, in her statement, in her facts and her helpless tone, so much potential for guilt for each of us that I am instinctively defensive. I waver, my acknowledgment unvoiced.

"What I can't figure out is why I could never be with him without secretly not wanting to be with him, and then I just wanted to come here with you. Wanted it like I used to want Christmas as a kid."

Afraid to let her berate herself harder, I reach over to comfort her, stroking her hair with my fingers. There are pulpy knots in her hair where it has become snarled in our lovemaking.

She sniffs. "I'm sorry. I really am. I didn't know I was going to be like this. But I just feel so fuckin' miserable."

Through my fingertips, I can feel her renewed struggle with her tears.

In my sexual hunger, can I have missed the signals that it would hurt her like this?

"Maybe," I try, "you just needed to let somebody know how lousy you're feeling."

"But I'm so embarrassed, so sorry, to be crying like this. I certainly didn't shed any tears when the engagement broke up."

"Maybe the engagement didn't mean as much to you as you think."

"It meant something. And not just because it was a long time between offers."

I listen silently, fearful that any words I use at this point will be inappropriate as soon as they issue from my thoughts.

"You don't know how much other crap there is in my life."

"I didn't mean it to sound that way." It is, I realize, a clumsy apology best dropped. I wait.

We are silent, listening to each other's next breath.

"Maybe," she announces to the darkness, "I only did this with you tonight to prove to myself that I'm over him."

"Is that what you did?"

"I don't know. If it is, I'm sorry."

"So am I."

She turns away.

I let her go.

From her side of the pillow, she says, "You don't have to worry about any of this being your fault. It was all the liquor they were serving."

"You barely touched anything."

"Because I was drinking some wine I skipped my medication. And now it's caught up with me. As fucking usual."

"What kind of medication?"

"For depression. Uni-polar mood disorder."

"I didn't know."

"You don't wear any bandages."

"I guess not."

"It's always there. Waiting. Any time you give it an inch of low serotonin."

"I'm sorry."

"Not half as sorry as I fucking am."

She swallows hard. "I didn't bring any medication in my purse. Took too little before I went out. Wanted it left there in the bathroom until after I got home. Wanted to prove that it couldn't stop me from going out and having a good time like my friends."

"And I'm the reason you didn't get home."

"That's not it at all."

"What then?"

"I wanted to go without it. Truly believed I could. Believed I could get away with it. And it just grinds the shit out of every Jesus day of my life."

Chastened by her confession to regret my suspicions she is toting baggage of her past relationships, I lean over and pull her back to me. She comes easily, letting her head sink heavily into my shoulder.

Friends.

I try to spill enough of my caring into her that she will never again have to feel sorry about anything in her life; refusing to recognize that there can be any limitations to what my caring can achieve; refusing to acknowledge I could be reading her feelings through my feelings, winnowing fresh sentiment from the chaff of my own loneliness.

She begins to talk in unconnected spurts about her life, telling how she has risen through her law firm, how she likes country and western music and new cookbooks and old Burt Reynolds movies.

With each piece of her portrait I become more aware of the wide differences in our values, situations, lifestyles, aspirations; aware that this is now becoming more than us simply tumbling into the sack; and I become fearful that I am committing some aching error, some weak and selfish error. Because I cannot now protect her from her own insecurities. If I withdraw any inch of my emotion from her, how, afterwards, can I possibly prevent her from thinking that I have used her for casual sex and then rejected her when she has trusted me enough to confess her secret problems? So I listen carefully in the darkness to this woman whose name I have never heard before this evening; realizing all the more how easily she can be wounded by my least indication of regret.

In the ambiguity and obscurity of the final wilting hour before dawn I somehow become sure that I can carry her through to the morning that is certain to arrive, sure that I can carry both of us through to it.

21

iding the elevator up to her floor felt so much like a familiar business trip activity that I did not have to think about the consequences of what I was doing until she appeared at my knock on her door.

She waited, her questioning obvious in her fatigued eyes.

She was wearing a T-shirt, faded baggy sweat pants.

I feared that, with her changing her dress from dinner, she had yielded to her fatigue. I feared she lacked the stamina to keep pace with my explanation, and tried to get to it as quickly as possible. "I wanted to come back."

"Why?" she demanded dryly.

"Tearing around," I replied. "Escaping. I'd like to stop."

I watched, and I was relieved as much by revealing that fragment of recent intimacy as by the concern I found rippling in her face. We had—my ungainly plea, her clumsy caring—somehow validated ourselves.

She stepped back, inviting me to follow with stray fingers.

I trailed her into the centre of her room, our individual resolves meshed in the muffled impact of the door closing behind us.

When she turned to face me, I told her, "I lied about my wife's suicide because it was full of people drowning me in sympathy or rejecting me because they didn't want to be near it."

"And you didn't want that from me?"

"I didn't want you to have to pay for them."

For several breaths I merely stood beside her, intuitively knowing not to approach her physically or verbally until she digested my words. In the glass eye of the television set, I could see our distorted reflection.

"I've never wanted anyone else to be involved in my problems," I confessed. "I was trying to do this without involving you. It seemed unfair to you. I made it worse. I'm sorry."

Without glancing down, I reached for her hand, hoping at least to join our reflected image. My fingers bumped hers.

"I've never felt old enough to have a dead wife. I want to let someone into my life again. I'd like it to be you."

She stepped away from me, inhaled fully, blew out slowly through her pursed lips; an obvious medley of relief and disquiet.

Some lines you cross knowing there is no safe way back.

I stayed silent; trying not to question her in word or action or attitude because I sensed she was questioning herself about allowing my return. Was she tracing other hurts she had suffered in her relationships back to a weak moment of forgiveness such as this?

She drifted to the nearest chair, settled tidily, lifted an open bottle of mineral water from a loose stack of paperwork on the side table, took a mouthful.

I was quick to sit on the corner of the mattress, facing her, wanting my presence in her room to carry our shared consent and not require further instruction or permission.

Her response did not come from the same direction.

"Get your big call?" she asked.

It seemed best to follow her. I nodded. "Done."

She wiped the back of her wrist at her dry cheeks and fore-head as if they were wet. Drank some more from her bottle, as if intent on absorbing our complications into her activity with her hands so that we could move beyond them for the moment.

In mild mockery of herself she said, "I'm trying to drink a lot of water to dilute the wine. That's the first time I've drunk that much at dinner. Since some stupid staff party last Christmas. I'm up too early every morning to ever drink at all at dinner."

I wanted to contribute, but was confused about what was required; I still carried the static of the telephone line in my thoughts; it made everything sound hollow and required added concentration. I realized that I must be both men, the one out there tied to the money and the one here in this room with her.

Categorically, she asked me, "You get through Christmas?"

I hesitated, listening to my own breath. My murmuring heart.

"First Christmas after I got divorced really sucked," she contin-ued. "And I've seen it be a real horror show for terminal patients and their families when they deteriorate into the final stretch to die a couple of days before Christmas. Not the best time for any kind of grieving."

In the chilly air conditioning, I waited intently for her to say more.

She shifted her eyes onto me in alert inquiry. "You want to make me into yet one more person that you can't talk to?"

"That what you think about me?"

"Tell me I'm wrong. Tell me there's anyone in your life right now who's not on the shut-out list."

I was overwhelmed with a sense that something I had not yet received was going to be taken away from me before it was placed in my hands.

I straightened, arched my shoulders back to pull the stiffness from them. "I think," I admitted, "I just pretended it wasn't Christmas. It's hard to recall. It's like nothing in me has been working to record any memories for the last while. Like looking through a video recorder, but forgetting to press the record button."

"Jesus," she whispered.

In the ungoverned dip of her eyes, I could sense how my honesty had touched her. I knew my next words must be absolutely truthful not to hurt her.

"Stay with me tonight," I said.

"Why?"

"I need you."

Through the still air between us I felt her fill with fragile tension.

"Do you really mean that?" she asked. "Or are you just making a good-night grab at me?"

"I don't want to leave you," I told her, hoping it would be enough, hoping by it I will be insulating her from the money where I too often must mould halfway commitments out of halfway uncertainties.

"But do you mean it?" she asked again.

I knew it had not been enough. There was, I sensed, no safe answer that would protect her. I answered as gently as I was able, even though it left me feeling vulnerable, sounding impoverished. "Yes."

She overtook me with her succinct question. "Is this where we were headed all through dinner?"

"What do you want me to tell you?"

"The truth."

"The truth is I don't seem to know how to answer questions

like that these days." I lunged after feelings that fled from me. "The truth is that up until I came back and knocked on your door I've felt like I've been walking around in someone else's life."

From her reaction, I recognized I had tried harder than I should have.

She drew back in her chair far enough to frown into my face. "What about afterwards? When we get back to Canada?"

It pulled at me like receding surf. "You're not remarried, are you?"

She huffed her rueful amusement. "To have time for that you first have to have time for a life. How could I ever find time for a life when I work seventy hours a week."

"Sorry."

She looked slightly past me to some noise tripping up the corridor on the other side of the door so that I could only watch the straining whites of her eyes. "If it's only for tonight. Can we do that?"

I was disoriented by her sudden digression. "Why?"

She told me, "To do this, I need to know that it stays here. It's not that I would regret it. It's that I become a different person when I'm back at the hospital, and I don't have much chance to process my personal feelings when I'm that different person who has to take care of so many sick and dying patients. Whether I want to or not, my patients suck mountains of emotion out me, and more often than not I have next to nothing left over for my personal life. I've had things like this end badly because of that. To do this, I need to know that you understand that I can't promise anything from here to back there."

I waited, trying to conceal that she had caused me to stumble. "Can we do that?"

"Yes," I told her, nodding against my stirrings of distant doubt.

She suggested, "Why don't we try starting from where we left off. Why don't you kiss me one more time and then we can get that out of the way."

I slid along the edge of the bed to her chair, stood, leaned in to her.

She shifted to receive my kiss as I brushed my lips against hers. Acutely, I was anxious about the sufficiency of my caring, afraid it would be like drawing on some muscle gone weak from lack of exercise. In the little thought I had given to it in past months, I had allowed that I would somehow arrive at this situation at some indistinct time in the future. I had tried to imagine it out of my past, like making a quilt from scraps of memory. I had never gotten further than assuming there would be an easy transition after a series of evenings or encounters smoothed out with conversation; with days or weekends in between to think, adjust, let my emotions recalibrate so that I would not harm someone I cared for with incomplete response.

I stroked the back of her neck with my worrying fingers because I was hesitant to put my hands elsewhere.

She pulled away. "I'm not going to be very good at this."

"There's no one at home?" I inquired, sitting back down on the edge of the mattress.

"There's an oncologist," she allowed. "We go out to dinner once a month or so. And I bring him home sometimes. But we're used to each other. It's comfortable." She shrugged pliantly. "Besides, we're both so overworked we're half asleep through it most of the time."

I was motivated by her honesty to reciprocate. "This is the first time I've done this," I said quietly. "Since my wife." I tried to make it sound less large by not adding anything further.

"I didn't want to ask."

"I would have lied," I admitted. I sat back on the wrinkled bedspread for several seconds, weighing out the grains of my reply. "I want it to be you. What do you want?"

"Not," she confessed, "getting hot and heavy and having you rip my clothes off. I can't do that. Why don't you let me get undressed in the bathroom. You can get undressed here, wait for me in bed. Somehow I'll feel better if we're both undressed at the same time. No pretend passion. No lies."

She pushed to her feet.

I wanted to say something reassuring, but remained silent, fearful that any words I did not feel to the bottom with similar conviction would be graceless as soon as they issued from my thoughts.

She stepped away decisively.

I began to say something I judged apt.

By then she had already gone into the bathroom. Closed the door.

I waited. The abrupt isolation sobered me, blotting the alcohol's woolly edges from my thoughts. I feared I was betraying my wife if I was too eager and did not maintain sufficient guilt to house her memory.

I stretched, sore with fatigue. I let my head loll back.

Judith's psychiatrist had explained that she probably thought she was going to commit suicide like a movie star in an old movie. Gulp down a handful of pills and drift off to sleep with violins. Although I cannot cast the words, I speak through all of it within myself in bitter dialogue with the voice. About how both the Luvox and the Effexor would cause terrible seizures and convulsions. About how both drugs spread quickly through the bloodstream. One of their main benefits for therapeutic use. Except for her, they would have burned through her arteries like wildfire, knocking her life out from under her. Permitting no second chances to change her mind, no mercy, no space for regrets.

I mislaid minutes. Going away into my thoughts.

She emerged from the bathroom wrapped in a large white towel.

She scolded me. "You're supposed to be undressed in bed."

I tried to make my expression apologetic.

"Unless you want me to feel really humiliated standing here in this goddamn towel."

Contrition, and smallness, rose in me like fever.

I shucked my jacket, kicked my shoes, pulled off everything else. Stepping to the head of the bed, I yanked down the bedspread and dropped in under the sheet, looked over to her.

I let my eyes run up her shiny white shins to the hem of the towel.

I have had to make shaky truces with the voice, not in perpetuating my love of my dead wife beyond her death, but in bearing my blame of it into all else that I do. But how could I be expected to maintain those vows and carry that blame into this?

As if sensing my misgiving, she seemed to move only on the balls of her feet and was at the bed before I realized it. She dropped a strip of condoms on the bedside table. She peeled the towel away from her body and let it drop to the floor.

In my mind, I tried to see her luscious and febrile, willing it to be simple to give myself over to a mutual rhythm of desire.

Instead, she was angular and vulnerable, and I found myself rushing to cradle her in softer yearning.

I allowed my eyes to fall from her face to her freckled shoulders and breasts, to her tangle of hair, to a blue mole on her thigh.

She followed my eyes downward with her own.

I flinched to realize that I had made her self-conscious of some perceived imperfection.

She turned off the light, cloaking herself in darkness, slipped dutifully between the sheets, leaving me wanting still to see her naked.

Fleetingly, lust flowered in my loins; flowed into the vacant cracks inside me between my thoughts and my inner voices.

Then, as the darkness snatched away my image of her body, my desire receded. And I was reminded of what we were, together in this distant hotel room in this distant city.

I let her recline beside me for several breaths before obediently sliding my arm under her shoulders and pulling her to me. She rolled against me tentatively.

The sheets smelled of bleach and had stiff creases where they had been pleated and pressed.

Her skin was warm within the cool sheets, on the cold pillow.

Lightly, I brushed my lips along the nape of her neck, trying to reassure us both with the fragile contact.

I found myself saying, "I feel like I'm trying to get to you on the other side of the room with all of the lights out. I know where I want to go, but I can't see in the dark and can only feel my way along and I keep bumping into everything."

"When I was five years old," she told me, "I climbed out my bedroom window one night. In the summer. Late. I went up and down our street. Looking at the houses. At people watching television in their living rooms. Or just seeing darkened rooms. Black windows. It frightened me. And the more I stayed out there going from one house to the next, the more it frightened me no end. Until, eventually, I just became paralyzed with fear. I rolled up into a ball on somebody's front porch. And stayed there, rolled up, until they found me in the morning."

"What scared you so much? Getting lost?"

"No. I got terrified because the night-time and the darkness were everywhere. For some reason I had the idea that the night-time and the darkness were only in the places where I was sleeping. Not everywhere else. When I became aware that it came to everyone else, everywhere else, it terrified me."

"Because it was dark everywhere?"

"Because there was no escape."

Slowly, I advanced my hand across the bony ridge of her shoulder and let my fingers float through the hollow of her throat to settle into the velvety skin over her heart. Her heartbeat murmured up through that fragile flesh to my fingertips with what I imagined was a plea for me not to invade it.

She caught her breath in a gentle gasp.

Her body and her breath took me back to my first summer with Judith; coming out of the shower to see her standing at the ironing board in her bra and panties, ironing a skirt so we could go out to dinner. The radio filling our bedroom with the song "Love Has Gone" in the way that the song seemed to be on every rock radio station everywhere that summer, like wallpaper in the air of our humid summer days. Judith singing along with the radio, "love has gone ... love has gone ...," lagging behind the melody when it climbed out of her range. The sudden burst of the telephone ringing into the music; Judith leaning to grab the receiver, knocking the ironing board; the upright iron skidding down the length of the board and bouncing against her hip on its way to the floor; burning an angry crescent the size of a small banana into her unblemished skin. She yelped. Jumped back. The wound with her for more than a month because her waistbands kept catching the dressing, tearing the face of the weeping burn. And how careful I was when I held her, when we undressed each other. When we made love. My quiet caring for her concentrating my life into tranquil breaths where I could lay aside my other thoughts and be mindful only of her. Of us together.

Rolling onto my side to embrace Wilma, my caring followed

a familiar habit of warning my fingers of an unseen burn on her hip.

But I found, when I did so, I let her become confused with Judith, and misplaced my wanting of her.

At the same time, I was deeply tempted to soft passive motions with Wilma to escape from my problems into her arms, hiding from my pressure-cooker life by letting her give me more than I gave in return. Letting her minister to my body with her body.

In persistence as much as passion, I restored Wilma by unfolding her with my deliberate touching.

I struggled to contain my impulse to apologize for having to work so hard at it because I recalled what it had done to me each time I had heard Judith tell me that she was sorry for her inability to respond to me, how it had made me feel selfish for wanting her to rise to my passion, how it had left me feeling powerless to help her. And, in doing so, I now began to understand what it had cost Judith—in sadness and relinquished hope and surrender to her illness—to apologize so repeatedly.

I let Wilma push my face lower, then lower still. I traced the geography of her body with my mouth, locating the centre of her heat, igniting her pleasure, fanning it with my tongue. Letting her teach me that I must be cruel in digging my fingers into her thrusting hips without concern for remembered wounds, grabbing hard, pulling tight, holding back nothing, until the darkness everywhere no longer separated us.

22

Where was I now? How much behind me, how much to go?

Alone in my hotel room, I measured out my questions in shallow steps within a meticulous circuit between the table and the bed. Suit pants and clean white shirt, but still in my bare feet. The coffee in my cup grown cold while I showered and shaved. Pursuing my analysis of my progress and options; look forward to what I might learn, and then look backward to what I already knew; shine a flashlight beam out into the darkness to catch what might await, or stand in the light and see what shadows where thrown behind me. Determined to prepare myself. Lunch with Stanley and Benjamin Lim loomed as the hour played out.

I could feel my instincts returning. The meeting required I be absolutely certain, in advance, of what I must obtain, what I could give away that was of value, what I could throw away because it lacked value—a continuous process of clarifying and re-clarifying, like distilling drops of purified perception from a swirling vapour of ambition and fear.

I discarded my curling pages of handwritten notes on the smooth, undisturbed bedspread.

An hour after dawn, with brilliant sunlight eating at the edges of the drawn drapes, she twitched awake when I began to slide from beneath the sheet.

She clicked on the bedside lamp and we got out of bed on opposite sides, dressing with our backs to each other. Twisting to pull on my socks, I caught a glimpse of her reflection in a mirror as she pulled clothes from an open suitcase on the floor. I saw only a flash of her putting on her bra by bending forward into it and hooking the clasps behind her back; yet, in that instant, could not help remembering how the last woman I had seen dressing, Judith, always did it so differently, joining the clasps in front beneath her breasts and then sliding the cups around and raising her arms through the shoulder straps. Like a thread that, for a few seconds, connected a single point in my present to a single point in my past while skipping everything in between.

We seemed to finish simultaneously, turning to each other in unison.

"Would you let me leave first?" she asked, slipping on her wrist watch. "I can go down and get some coffee."

I did not understand, questioned her tacitly with my look.

"I just don't want to be alone in the room when you go out the door," she explained. "Having someone fuck me. And then walk out the next morning."

"We could have coffee together."

"Let me have some time. Okay?" She glanced into the mirror, filled with a yellow ball of light from the lamp, and pushed at her hair down over her temples with her palms. "I just need a little space for my feelings." She pulled her lips into a thin smile for me. "No regrets about last night."

I smiled back to reassure her, attempting to cover my hesitation and discomfort. It came out sketchy.

She noticed.

I stepped to her and placed my hands on her shoulders gently.

She pecked me on the cheek hurriedly and began to pull away.

"Later?" I asked.

She slowed with indecision. "I don't know. I don't know right now if I'll want to."

"Okay," I assured her.

Barely, she nodded, then looked deliberately at my hands still on her shoulders.

I let them fall away.

She went to the door, opened it and walked out, closing it behind her before there was time for any further words.

I stood alone in the silent room. Listening just in case.

∽∾

In foreign hotel rooms, decompressing from the stress of business meetings, but a long way from anything familiar, I always had some sense, lifted from old detective movies, of being on the lam. Being holed up before the showdown.

As I had on previous occasions, waiting in previous hotel rooms, I reminded myself that the one secret I had learned about life during my severe apprenticeship to the money was that more mature and more successful and more settled people did not know any more about how to organize their lives and make their decisions than I knew. They also suffered the same fears of the unknown, and the same sense of powerlessness, every time something they had paid to learn with past perseverance and sacrifice no longer worked in yet another new crisis. The secret I had learned was that, like me, everyone else made up their life as they went along.

တက္ကသ

They were waiting for me over tall glasses of ice tea at a table in the corner of the hotel dining room.

Stanley, smiling eagerly, waved me over into a chair.

Benjamin Lim was twice our age, soft-faced, soft-spoken. Blooming in a lime-green golf shirt.

Stanley ushered us through a speedy introduction, a quick trade of nodding smiles and hasty handshakes, swapped business cards, concluding with his hurried reminder, "And I've given Benny my sworn oath that he won't miss his tee-off time."

We caught a waiter, ordered sandwiches, settled back.

Hoping to illustrate my situation and my needs in a series of steps where I could safely test support for each before moving on to the next, I met Benjamin Lim's expectant grin by opening with, "Thank you for fitting us in on short notice. We have a proposition I think will make it worthwhile."

Benjamin Lim hop-scotched ahead by several exchanges. "Stanley tells me you need money."

I felt the safe middle ground drop away. Challenged to jump straight into my request with no chance to cushion it within a convincing argument. Left wide open to Benjamin Lim's initial acceptance or rejection. My future boiled down to another man's yes or no.

I sensed my only option was to match his pace. "Yes."

"How much?"

"Ninety million."

Benjamin Lim pursed his lips in appreciation. "That's a lot."

"Yes." Elude any impediment arising from debate of that judgment.

"How long do you need it?"

"One or two days. A week maximum."

"When?"

"We need the commitment in forty-eight hours. We'll need to draw funds in a few weeks."

"And what do you have for collateral?"

"Bonds. One-year maturities. Bangkok Commercial Bank. Face value a hundred million."

Benjamin Lim paused, flicked his eyes to Stanley for confirmation. Stanley nodded, fixed and positive and sure; committing his personal credibility to mine.

No turning back now.

Benjamin Lim leaned away, took me in carefully. "Why?"

It was obvious that Stanley had already detailed the deal and the players, the score, the potential for profit. Benjamin Lim's piercing question, I recognized, had nothing to do with gathering the facts. It was critical that my answer provide a measuring of my own competence and command of the situation, and ensure that my views were congruent with Stanley's because it was Stanley that Benjamin Lim would trust throughout this, not me. I was only along for the ride if I could prove that my participation and skills added value. I stated my facts concisely, hoping that the punchy delivery would testify to our unity and underscore that I was unclouded in my conviction of their success.

"Mezzanine finance. To pay for the bonds until they're resold in an arbitrage."

My words landed on the table.

Our sandwiches arrived.

Benjamin Lim immediately flipped open half of the fried egg sandwich on his plate, basted it with ketchup. Squeezed it back together, lifted it to his mouth. Ripped out a thick bite. Chewing, he commanded, "Tell me about it."

I felt myself having to hang on harder than usual to what I knew best because so much remained stubbornly unknown.

I laid out the backwards domino effect quickly, leaving my own sandwich untouched. "Our financing depended on a substantial credit line from Bank of South Asia. Amsterdam Bank didn't appreciate us snatching the deal out from under their noses after they'd already pre-sold it at fire-sale prices below market. So they threatened to dump a lot of BSA stock. And BSA couldn't afford to take a hit on their equity because they're already suffering from a bundle of write-downs on a lot of bad business they wrote last year."

I knew to deliberately avoid the Mayfield Hotels mortgage bonds to prove that I understood it was a matter that risked loss of face, and would only be discussed by Stanley and Benjamin Lim in private. ·

"And now, of course," Benjamin Lim asserted, mouth full, chewing intently, "Amsterdam has come calling on Bangkok Commercial to save them by taking the bonds off their hands."

"Yes."

"But at a steep price."

"Yes."

"So what difference would it make even if you had the money now?"

Before I could answer, Benjamin Lim redirected the question to Stanley with a flick of his fingers as he prepared the remaining half of his sandwich with ketchup. "Stanley?"

"Paris," Stanley began eagerly, then stopped, corrected himself. "We."

Our shared problems coalescing into shared purpose, shared commitment, shared future.

"We've met with Bangkok Commercial. Paris has renegotiated

the contracts to include clauses to make the bonds non-transferable. So Amsterdam Bank can't snap them up and unload them by spinning them out to their pre-sales."

"Do you have these contracts?" Benjamin Lim inquired of me pointedly.

"Yes." I did my best to augment Stanley's narrative by confidently tapping the briefcase beside my chair.

"If the bonds are non-transferable, how do you get rid of them?"

"I've worked out a series of interlocking trusts with Sanoh Sajjakul, managing director at Bangkok Commercial. We hold the non-transferable bonds in the trusts. When the trusts are settled and locked, they'll get the same Moody's rating as Bangkok Commercial prime paper. Then we issue Moody's-rated asset-backed participation certificates to investors behind us."

"Reselling a hundred-million-dollar syndication can take time. Usually longer than a few days."

"Normally, yes. But not in this case. We really only have one client to sell to. Amsterdam Bank. They've got to have those bonds, or our equivalent certificates, to make good on all their pre-sales. They've got to take all of the certificates off our hands. In one sale. Immediately. Even if they lose a few dollars. Otherwise they risk standing out there in the markets with nothing in their hands. They have to defend against claims for non-delivery and lawsuits for breach. And they're embarrassed far beyond anything they'd ever be prepared to put up with."

"Of course."

"Yes."

"So," Benjamin Lim confirmed, "you need enough cash to pay for the bonds to put them into the trusts. Then you pay back the cash out of your sales of the asset-backed participation certificates. Which is immediately."

"Exactly."

Benjamin Lim swallowed the last of his sandwich, dug at the corners of his mouth with a napkin to clear them of ketchup. He dropped the napkin onto his plate. Blankly, he looked at us, back and forth, drumming his fingers on the table. He opened his mouth, inhaled, making us wait for it, then announced, "Your trusts pledge the collateral to us. Against one hundred million in bonds, we will give you ninety million. You have two banking days. You repay ninety-one million. Or you forfeit the bonds. Forfeit the participation certificates. Forfeit everything."

Some times with the money, it seemed the greater the amount, the fewer the words.

Gradually, I tried to ease out my reply. "In annualized interest, that's just a little over two hundred per cent return on your investment."

"And," Benjamin Lim smiled blandly, "you have a choice. Seek financing elsewhere."

I glanced to Stanley, who shrugged me off, unable to do any more at this juncture because it was family. For the next minutes, my future was in my own hands.

I felt I would fade in Benjamin Lim's measurement of me if I did not voice sufficient scepticism.

"What's China Success Leasing doing with that much loose cash? By anyone's standards that's an awful lot to leave invested at low yield on overnight float. And your credit committees wouldn't want that much siphoned off the operating lines for a single risk."

Benjamin Lim blocked off any fresh discussion with his colourless silence.

The only option for keeping the deal in play was to move forward, learn more, ask a neutral question that would not incite further discord.

"Do we," I asked politely, "borrow directly from China Success Leasing?"

"No."

Not the answer I expected.

"Who, then?"

"You will sign a contract and pledge all collateral to a company called Great Golden Holdings. The funds will be transferred from several numbered accounts from two private banks in the Cayman Islands."

"What's the source of the funds?"

"I'm not able to disclose that information."

"So the money transfers into our deal from unidentified sources."

"Yes."

"But when we pay it back to Great Golden Holdings it will be clearly identified as investment proceeds from our bond deal."

"Yes."

"Nice and neat and clean."

"Yes."

I tried to make my voice sound careful rather than challenging, fearful of letting his fragile lifeline slip from our fingers. "Should we have any concerns about the source of the money?"

"Concerns?"

Benjamin Lim's single word returned like a closed door.

I shrugged. Indicating the obvious implications.

What you didn't say more important than what you said.

Benjamin Lim took it up. "Will your banks, Mr. Smith, cause problems by thinking that the money is being laundered?"

"They might." I let my words stay rough around the edges without any smoothing from further explanation.

"And do you think the money is being laundered?"

"I might." Then I saw his eyes register a diminished impression of my nerve, and I added, "No. Not at all."

He paused, satisfying himself. He continued. "I'm too old to take offence to things said in business dealings. Outrage is for younger men who let their emotions cloud their decisions."

Silence. Humidity overpowering the air conditioning in our tight corner.

"You ask no questions of our cash," Benjamin Lim confirmed, "we ask no questions of your deal."

I felt it sing urgently within me, how the seduction of the money was not in what it would allow you to buy, but in what it would make someone else sell. In how it could flow around risk and mistrust and objections like water flowing around polished rocks. Allowing you to reach into the future and control the outcome of events yet to come; but at a cost of bringing tomorrow's fears to settle like silt into the unused spaces of your life.

"If the Cayman banks will issue a SWIFT interbank transmission or a sworn affidavit attesting their satisfaction with the source of the deposits, we'll take care of the rest."

"You're sure?" Benjamin Lim asked. "We must have no problems from Bangkok Commercial."

"We'll guarantee them that the Cayman source is tax planning," I stated. "Holding your international dollars outside of taxable jurisdictions for international investments."

"Which," Benjamin Lim affirmed, "is exactly the case."

"Taking care of those details is our part of the deal. You can depend on us."

Benjamin Lim nodded slowly, spoke softly. "Stanley says you have honour."

I could feel it coming back. How tough situations and tough

decisions stretched me; how they accelerated my life; how they made me reach beyond what was familiar; accumulating, sometimes in a day, years of experience, knowledge, confidence.

"And," Benjamin continued, consulting a broad-banded Rolex on his wrist, "we must leave now if Stanley is to drive me to the golf course on time."

Stanley moved in to smooth it out. "Well, Paris?"

What else was there to do?

I nodded.

We shook hands all round.

They hustled out.

I remained standing by the empty table.

At the centre of my universe, I operated in free-fall, racing to pawn my release from failure; the heat of their hands staying on my hand.

∽∾

Slouched in armchairs, Stanley and I painted the corner of my hotel room with our tired voices, the last afternoon sun pulsing through the window to us from its frayed hole in the hazy sky.

Outside, the streets below were loud, their clamour vibrating through the window glass. I let my gaze wander down to the congested intersection, to the masses of people jerking by in vehicles, on motorbikes, packing the hot dusty sidewalks in impatient knots. I could not help imagining the fabric of their lives, happiness and hunger and heartbreak. It was as if I could hear the babble of their thoughts, feel their sea of emotions, boiling upwards on the rising heat. The sensations reminded me I had let my life be pummelled into myopia; and they renewed my desire for what I did not have.

Within the room, our discussion circled back on itself in a

loop, like a tape recording repeatedly rewound and replayed. We volleyed our words, as if sufficient velocity in our discussion would sustain us in our approaching actions.

"At least it's a real offer, Paris."

"If we take it."

"Solves your problems and lets you deliver to Bangkok Commercial before the deadline."

I reminded, "I'm really going to have to sell the hell out of it back in Toronto."

"It's not some bullshit transfer of a million bucks a week through some nominee account. It's a major bond deal. Funds straight in and straight out. Your company's too small to be expected to have that much cash around. You always have to deliver from an investor syndicate behind you."

"Did you know that's what he was going to offer?"

"No. When I began to lay it out for him, he hinted at some type of special arrangements. Maybe I suspected then. But I wasn't sure about what I was suspecting."

"Ninety-one million, Stanley. We have to pay back ninety-one million. Which means we have to resell the bonds for at least ninety-one million. Which means we've got to buy the bonds from Bangkok Commercial for less than ninety-one million."

"Even at ninety-one million on the flip, you can offer Bangkok Commercial ninety million on the buy. That means Bangkok Commercial sells us the bonds at a ten per cent discount and pays us ten per cent interest to raise their money compared to Amsterdam gouging them for thirteen per cent. And that still leaves a spread of one million in the middle to pay the cost of the ride to China Success."

"Plus we earn all of the sales commissions."

"You got that right."

"But there's still a huge obstacle. I've still got to get my directors back in Toronto to agree to sign the contract from Great Golden Holdings. And they'll never do it. As soon as they get a whiff of the Cayman details, they'll run for the hills."

"Like Benny says, what choice do you have?"

"I don't see any other choice. But I think they will. They've got some other cards up their sleeves."

"Like Bahamas. Like Global Vest Banking with Albert Quan."

"Exactly."

Stanley absorbed my facts, leaned back, delivered his pronouncement smoothly. "I wouldn't be so sure of the long-term survival rate of that deal."

"How so?"

"I learned early on that Albert was a two-edged sword. He cut me into as many deals as he cut me out of. I was tired of walking into the office every morning never knowing which way the wind was blowing until I found out from him."

From the way he tapered his account I recognized he was not going to explain further. I shrugged through it. "For me, I'm still stuck with some backroom Bahamas deal back in my office, my senior partner."

"Then your guys are already bending all the rules."

"Sounds like they've already agreed to be whores," I agreed. "Now we're all just haggling about the price."

"And compared to a dead deal, you've got a hell of a price for them here."

"Something tells me they'll drop the phone as soon as I mention it."

"So better not do it over the phone."

"What's my other choice?"

"Next flight out, if I were you."

"Take me twenty-four hours to get back to Toronto."

"I'll still need two or three days this end. I can fly up to Hong Kong tomorrow morning. Nail down Benny at breakfast. But then I'll need to sit on things up there until the lawyers hammer out the contract."

I felt the need to reduce our tempo, check my bearings. "Stanley, why are you doing this?"

"A lot of money. Finder's commission from China Success. Probably about ten thousand a day for a week's work."

"What else?"

"I'm not the one to ask. I'm on the outside looking in. You're stuck in the middle. Why are you pushing yourself so hard? Why not just give in? Let your guys work it out with their backroom Bahamas deal."

"I gave my word to Bangkok Commercial, to Sanoh Sajjakul. If I go back on it..."

"Not your fault. You got blindsided by your own people."

"And then what?"

"Resign. Go home. Take a few weeks off."

"And what about Bangkok Commercial? Sanoh Sajjakul?"

"They'll recover."

"But I won't."

"Why not?"

"If I don't exist in my commitments, I don't exist at all in this life. You stick to one promise at a time, one person at a time."

Stanley waited.

"Besides," I added, "what am I buying if I throw this deal away?"

"What," Stanley countered, "are you buying if you sell yourself in Hong Kong for cash laundered in Cayman?"

"I'm doing something instead of nothing."

"And that's somehow better?"

"Yes."

Appraising me, Stanley commented, "Something's changed since you were in Bangkok last summer."

"You can't just stand back and watch when things are falling apart. You've got to do something, you've got to keep trying no matter what. I've learned that from someone."

"Who? Some senior partner?"

"My wife."

✖

Alone in my room, I scooped up the layers of paperwork that had now become my future, squashing them into my briefcase.

As I lifted the final sheets of paper in my fingers, I slowed. Stood still.

Wilma. The choice of direction of my life tilted off its axis. Not whether to go forward or back, but whether to go upstairs or down. My route straight back to the airport. My promise to her not to go straight back to her.

Judith. Guilt came like fog, soft at the edges, filling unguarded spaces. Slowly blocking out distance and perspective.

Regret returned like an old friend. I struggled to escape its familiar promise of false comfort.

All of the uncertainty in my life seemed concentrated in my next choices.

I was bound by some sense that I was neither finishing nor leaving.

At their edges, the sheets of paper in my fingers fluttered.

23

Going backward through the hours.

Twenty-four hours of flying while only turning the clock back through twelve hours of time zones, so I paid only half a day of difference for a full day of travel.

Spooky, living the same hours twice.

Arriving in Toronto was a leap from summer to winter, heat to snow. Jump time. As if I had lost half a year out of my life, gone to sleep one night in July and woken up the next morning to the icy grip of February, blown backwards from summer to the previous winter, with no memories to show for the months in between.

Riding from the airport to my office, I was stunned by the cold and wind-chill. As if it was forcibly sucking the tropical Asian heat from my bloodstream.

I pressed myself back into the corner of the taxi seat.

Shivered.

Carried along by the mid-afternoon bustle, I arrived at my office expecting Michelle's wide welcoming grin at reception. Then remembered she was on vacation. No matter. Kyle would be waiting. I knew better than to surprise Kyle, risk the inevitable gusts of annoyance and impatience; I had called him from the plane almost six hours ago. It had gone poorly. Several starts to my description of my bond solution cut off with impatient interruptions and jagged criticism. Tomorrow's results amputated today. Making no progress, I had censored the rest of the details myself to shield them from the doubt sown within my mind by Kyle's derision.

I nodded my way past the replacement receptionist, taking my curled message slips from their slot. I bumped my wheeled suitcase down the corridor, swung it into my office. Closed my office door and leaned back against it, appreciating the firmness against my stiff shoulder muscles, as I leafed through the message slips. The cramped notes blurred in my vision. I had slept a few hours on the plane, but only a fraction of what I needed because the flight had been full, busy, meal carts serving, people passing in the aisles, voices crackling into my skin-deep dreams. I was exhausted to the brink of nausea. I had to discard the notes on the corner of my desk, unread, stretching out my breathing to steady my stomach.

When I was composed and felt the floor return beneath my feet, I opened the door, continued up the corridor.

The emptiness waiting within my hollow home floated seductively at the fringe of my thoughts; it would require no energy to retreat there, not answer the phone.

But I knew on instinct I first had to get through this next part.

I spurred myself through the open door into Kyle's office.

Kyle was waiting.

Ted Dwyer was waiting.

Kyle waved me to a chair.

Some abbreviated greetings were scattered to the carpet as I took my seat.

Ted Dwyer spoke first. "Kyle informs me you've been a busy beaver over in Bangkok."

I nodded, knowing from their tone, from their postures, that it was not yet my turn to speak.

"You've been telling Kyle that you've got a restructured deal. Completely new. With Hong Kong players instead of Singapore players."

"There's more." I deliberately avoided a succinct confirmation, hoping to strengthen my arguments and my position by leaving a vacuum and causing a need for additional details. This, I hoped, would elevate me to the status of partner in the meeting rather than a subordinate reporting to them, all of the decision-making power concentrated in their hands.

I gauged some minimal success when Dwyer leaned back on the couch, dropped his hands off his lap, opening himself to listen. "So tell us."

I knew from past experience with Kyle to condense it. Make it nimble, flat-out quick. Get all of the details into play instantaneously. Make them take the bait in their eagerness to lambaste me. If I could make them bicker with me about the size of the deal, they had to consent that there was going to be a deal, and they forfeited their right to argue about whether a deal was needed or not.

"We owe Bangkok Commercial for the bonds on March tenth," I stated. "Bank of South Asia reneged on our financing because Amsterdam Bank threatened to dump their shares and punch the bottom out of their equity. Amsterdam took the easy way out and dumped the bonds into the market at a bargain-basement price. Then stuck it to Bangkok Commercial on the pricing. Meanwhile, we have to go sucking up to Amsterdam and get beat all to hell on spreads just to save our reputation in the markets and make good on the orders we booked." I paused to collect some emphasis, continued. "At which point Amsterdam sits back fat and happy because they just got laid twice, only had to pay once, and we both thank them for doing it to us."

Kyle led with, "Where do you fit into this wonderful tale?"

"I've gotten Bangkok Commercial to re-cut the bonds. Make them non-transferable so Amsterdam can't flip them. Instead, they settle the non-transferable bonds into trusts, and we get the bond trusts. Now Amsterdam has to come sucking up to us to save their own reputation in the markets and fill all the orders they booked. Which is a lot more than we ever sold. The entire hundred million, in fact. And we can turn around and issue asset-backed participation certificates to Amsterdam to help them out. At a profit, of course."

"Of course," Kyle repeated.

I pushed my tongue against the roof of my mouth to break up the rhythm between question and answer before it closed back in on me and made me appear to be defending my actions, waiting them out.

Our pace paused, but then seemed to skip a beat and accelerate against my attempts to control the tension and pull of our responses.

"Just where is it," Kyle inquired pointedly, "that we're getting all the cash to buy these non-transferable bond trusts?"

"New financing."

"New?"

"Hong Kong. Overnight money. We pledge the bonds as collateral. They give us ninety million to meet the payment price to Bangkok Commercial. Two days later, after we've refinanced to Amsterdam, we pay back ninety-one million."

"And who are our Hong Kong financing partners?"

"China Success Leasing."

"We're borrowing from China Success Leasing?"

"A Hong Kong holding company."

"Theirs?"

"I'm not sure. Probably."

"Then where's all the cash coming from? Their lines?"

"An investor group."

"Hong Kong?"

"Cayman."

"It's starting to sound just a lot more complicated from what you first explained."

"Let's wait," I urged, "until we get the contracts from the Hong Kong lawyers. The contracts should contain sufficient depth of diligence."

"To do what?"

"Shine enough light on the players and the cash to make it clear and raise us above all suspicion."

"I don't think so." Kyle flicked the backs of his fingertips on his desk several times, brushing away the funds, the request.

"Why not?" I demanded.

"I just don't."

"At least wait until we get the contracts from the Hong Kong lawyers. Let our lawyers look at them."

"Lawyers won't make any difference. Hong Kong, or the far side of Jupiter."

"How can you say that? I've just about killed myself pulling all of this together. It's good. It's solid. It works. And it's profitable."

Kyle's reply, and voice level, accelerated into spiky insistence. "That may be well and good. But that's not how it's going to work."

"Why not?"

"Because you're only thinking about the future of this firm, and you're only looking at everything, over the next ten days. You've got to learn how to think of things over the long term and look forward over the next ten years."

"And I haven't always made a contribution to the future of this firm, a major one?"

"Not with this re-cooked bond deal. Not today."

I refused to acknowledge Kyle's statements. If I allowed him to deny my efforts and discard my sacrifices, I permitted him to declare me valueless to the company. I ground my tired thumbs into the arms of the chair. My hate clustered in my chest like a second heart hammering against my first.

Passing seconds of silence flowed around our ankles like slow-moving water. I began to feel as if some perilous threat was about to rush out at me from the corners of the room outside my vision, but was afraid to take my eyes off them to look for it.

"There's always a bigger picture. You need a perspective. It comes with experience." A lofty contribution from Ted Dwyer.

Kyle slogged ahead, peeved, peppery. "Ted, please fill in the blanks for him."

Dwyer cleared his throat with a dry huff.

I swung my focus to the noise, stabbing at it with my concentration.

Dwyer raised his right hand, folded his fingers. "Everything hinges on three simple facts." He let his index finger pop up. "Number one. The Senate banking committee is willing to approve the sale of this investment bank." He straightened his middle finger. "Number two. But only to a domestic bank such as Atlantic Laurentide. Never to an evil foreign company who, God forbid, might make ugly ripples in our financial services sector." His final finger snapped to attention. "And number three. No matter what, the committee will never let this company collapse and create even uglier ripples in our financial services industry. Regardless of anything you may think is happening here."

Dwyer lowered his hand. "Understand?"

He waited deliberately on my unwilling nod before continuing by laying open his right palm. "We may not want to sell to a domestic bank like Atlantic Laurentide. For some very clear-cut reasons. So if we can't get what we want under the first two conditions—" He flipped his left palm over to coincide with his right. "—We have to create the third condition. Threat of failure."

Match point.

I knew I was now without further choice as to which facts I must raise in brittle reply, but held back my statements in latent fear. If I unleashed my information about the Bahamas scheme, I relinquished my only advantage.

They waited on me, their eyes joined on me.

In the window behind Ted Dwyer's head, snow began to blow against the glass. After Southeast Asia, the swirling flakes distracted me, held me like some hardly remembered magic trick.

I hesitated. Then I forced myself from my own sheltering shadows.

"The firm looks like it's about to fail as a result of a breached bond deal," I announced. "But the only suitor, Atlantic Laurentide, will be tied up in audits and evaluations for months before it coughs up an offer. Meanwhile we burn while Atlantic fiddles. And there's no other domestic bank willing to buy us. So it becomes expeditious for the Senate banking committee to make a rare exception and approve a quick sale to a foreign bank group. In the Bahamas."

I let my final syllables drag so I could measure their influence.

It was as if silence was being pumped into the room; as if, like stale air, it forced you to focus harder even though you could not see it.

"Global Vest Banking Corporation, in fact?" I released the name in a controlled tone, concealing my agitation, letting it do its own work, potent and poisonous.

Set the nail. It would draw the blow to it. And send its own cruelty back into the hammer.

Kyle glared.

Ted Dwyer chuckled appreciatively. "Well... well... well."

Kyle commented urbanely, "Curiosity killed the cat, Paris."

I pelted them with my facts. "You know Albert Quan. You've known him all your life since Yale. You engineered the deal with him. And with Amsterdam Bank in Geneva. Set it up in Bahamas. Has it got you enough of a threat of failure to scare the banking committee?"

Ted Dwyer nodded mildly. "Scaring the living Jesus out of them."

"So they'll approve?"

"If I'm any judge of it," Dwyer said, "by the end of March."

My innate sense of the game was blurred by their confirmation without the least dodging or denial. I could not tell how far my aggression went out towards them, or how far theirs came back to me—only that both aggressions met in the middle, latched on to each other, and refused to let go. It left me seeing in gulps of vision that took in their intentions for an instant, then shut them out.

"And what about my part?" I tried.

"You," Kyle emphasized drearily, "don't have a part."

"My deal? Bangkok Commercial Bank?"

"We drop it."

Of all the things I had ever seen for myself I had never imagined a time like this, a place like this.

"Why my deal?" I asked.

"Your deal had all the right ingredients." Kyle clasped his hands for emphasis. "Albert Quan agreed it would be profitable to cooperate. Regain some of the ground he and his family lost in the miserable markets over the last two years. And Amsterdam's investment banking division in Geneva was happy to help out. For a large slice of the pie."

"So you cooked up this whole thing, cooked up your own outside threat, and still let me hump it out in Singapore and Bangkok?"

Kyle shrugged it off blandly. "You do what it takes."

"That's awfully thin." I tired to stare him down.

He stared back without flinching. "How often have you told me during the last year that, even though you couldn't come in some days and couldn't make all of the meetings on this thing, I could always count on you to do what it takes."

Indignant, I refused to respond.

Kyle scratched at his nose vigorously, sniffed. "And your circumstances worked in our favour."

"Mine?"

"You've been unstable since your wife's suicide. It's been noticeable. Nothing personal. You've made rash decisions. Decisions without approval."

"In other words, I'm convenient."

"Wake up. You were convenient a year ago. You've been convenient every minute of every hour of every day for the last year."

"You targeted me as soon as I started missing meetings to stay home with my wife."

Kyle slipped away from my confrontation, refusing to be drawn into my argument and risk further admission. "It can't be me. I'm the senior partner, the managing partner. The Securities

Commission would crucify me. I'd be lucky to get out of prison, let alone out of the country."

"So I'll be forever known as the man who torpedoed Addison, Beaufort and Shulman."

"Some things are unavoidable."

"And I'm expendable."

"It's my firm. Not yours."

"But sustained the last couple of years by my achievements."

"Beggars mounted, ride their horses to death."

Biting back my resentment, I looked at myself looking at them. Only men sitting in an office. Talking. No fists raised, voices bridled. But their indifference spilling down on me like sand. Until I was no longer able to tell whether it was piling up around me or I was sinking into it. Only that I felt as if I was being buried alive.

Kyle resumed, a different tone, a different theme, loosely wagging his fingers. "You've got nothing to worry about."

"No?"

"You're finished at this firm. Finished in Toronto. But we'll take care of you. Give you a year's salary. Ted will call a few old friends, New York or London. Get you taken on at an insurance company or a bank with a fat package."

Ted Dwyer followed promptly with, "It's not as if you have any personal responsibilities at home any more that would keep you from relocating. If you don't mind me saying so."

I could feel how they were not sorry about their actions. Not even self-conscious. Not because they lacked emotion; but because they had learned they could not afford it in management decisions that required logic and objective focus. In their position, I could have made the same decisions. In similar circumstances, I had.

It was not betrayal.

It was business.

No one, I reminded myself, stayed in a burning building.

Still, the impact of it broke on me as if I had been caught in the face by a stray ball and had to blink the shock and wetness out of my vision before I could continue the game.

The voice pressed for attention, insinuating that I search out some obscure source of blame within myself. For a moment, my grasp slackened, slipped.

Kyle instantly perceived my hesitation, my pause to re-weave my words. He eased the solid set of his shoulders, leaned back in his chair, let his ankles cross. "It wasn't just you, Paris. The taxes are a big part of it. We sell out to Atlantic Laurentide at the end of the year, my equity's worth the best part of twenty million."

"And you want to hang on to it."

"I'm a founding partner. My cost on those partner shares was zero. So everything's a hundred per cent capital gain, a hundred per cent taxable."

From the side of the room, Ted Dwyer eased back into the conversation. "And that has some pretty nasty tax implications."

"Damn right," Kyle announced. "You think I want the goddamn government to help themselves to half of my twenty million?"

I had to agree. "It's a lot of tax."

"It's not the money," Kyle said wearily. "It really is the god-damn principle. Did the government risk anything to build this company? Did they put anything on the line? Was their name out there if we failed? And where the fuck were they in the lean years? All the nights and weekends we worked around the clock in the beginning." Kyle gathered his vehemence into a final pro-nouncement. "I'd rather throw the money down a sewer than see those shits get dollar one."

"And that," Ted Dwyer confirmed, "is the real beauty of the whole Bahamas setup. The buyout can be structured partly onshore and partly offshore"

When no other response would come to me, I said, "We've got about six hours left to get back to Bangkok Commercial. We have to let them know. I gave them my word."

"No," Kyle said stiffly. "Tell them no."

"No," Ted Dwyer added. "No."

As the weakened light of the winter afternoon seeped away, draping us in deepening darkness, I looked to one, the other. Waited for there to be some rift in their perceptions or opinions that would allow me to resume my argument.

When there was nothing, I stood. Left.

End of the line.

24

Both going to the airport. But separate flights. Our commitments and responsibilities indifferent to our desires. Wilma and I moved around the room in tandem. Trying to talk as she packed.

Our eye contact kept breaking as she twisted back and forth between her hangers and her suitcases. Each time it happened it slipped a joint in my thoughts, and I was afraid my intentions were spinning off into the vacant corners of the room; it made me mislay words I had tried to assemble and arrange in speaking them through within myself before coming up to knock on her door.

The room was bathed in tropical sunset, flaming neon light that was being consumed as it burned itself out. Unreal. Untrue. Reminding me that we were suspended in a fleeting interval before darkness, our circumstances temporary. Soon nothing will be clear or definite. Telling me that I had to hurry.

Her replies were tepid. "I'm out to London for six days. Not back to Toronto until the end of next week. You're all the way back on one long haul. It'll seem a lifetime travelling. For both of us. We can make good use of it. We can make last night seem like it happened in a past life."

"Or," I countered, "we can get together when you come home."

"For what?" She dropped her words in front of me.

"For us."

Her two suitcases were flipped open at the bottom of the bed. She side-stepped back and forth between them and the stacks of clothes and toiletries in ziplock sandwich bags lined up along both sides of the bedspread, across the pillows. "Then what? Talk about our memories of here?"

Standing at the base of her packing, I sensed she would toss aside any mention of intimacy that had passed between us if I pressed it. I treaded softly with superficial tribute. "Some time together," I tried, hoping my oblique reference was sufficient. "There. The same as here."

"My goddamn work never leaves time for anything else. Yours doesn't either. I've learned too many lessons the hard way."

"I'll make time for you."

"Don't make me feel sorry about myself."

"For last night?"

"For not being able to make the same promise. For being satisfied with spending my life at the hospital. On my patients."

"I let my career take over my life so I didn't have to face how little was left over. Is that the lesson?"

She yanked back on my challenge wickedly. "I'm not young and unattached."

"You said you weren't married."

"No. But I'm thirty-nine years old. I was married. And I've got ten-year-old twin boys."

"But you sound like you live alone."

She stopped folding a blouse. Her fingers lost their place. She had to shake it out and begin again. "I do. The guys live with their dad out in the suburbs. We've got a nanny for them there. And he keeps regular accountant's hours."

She had to stop talking while she pinned the blouse under

her chin, brought the arms into the centre of the fold with both hands. Finishing, she raised her eyes, questioning whether I would listen to more.

I nodded, urged her to continue.

She stepped to a suitcase, smoothed the folded blouse into a soft pile of clothes. Remained close to me. "They like it a lot better out there. School. Sports. The mall. I live in an old apartment a block behind the hospital. They show up some weekends when there's something they want to do downtown. But not otherwise. I don't even have cable on my television set. So I go out there to see them. Lot of times I get off at ten or eleven at night. If I don't have early rounds, I drive out there when there's no traffic. Bunk out. Get up in the morning with them and have breakfast with them. It's good time. They like it. Helps keep us close."

My unease zeroed in on issues of her sleeping arrangements, but I made myself accept that one night together, not much different than eating together because we were both hungry, did not entitle me to privileges of that proportion.

I tried to sound understanding. "I didn't know."

"That's just it," she said. "I'm halfway through my life. I've got a whole half of life you don't know anything about." She tried to make some picture of it with her hands. Gave up in frustration. "It's just too hard to take someone new into my life halfway through it."

"Try letting someone go out of your life halfway through it."

"Don't use that. It's pathetic."

My resentment churned unpleasantly.

I reached to her in appeal, letting my fingertips settle on her upper arms when she did not draw back. But was uncertain about what came next. So let go.

I felt the powerful pulling of wanting more. Unfamiliar in the thin gravity of making my life into wanting less.

"Her depression was like a concrete wall around her." I hated the humiliation of having to sow my secrets indiscriminately because the two of us were boxed in by so little time, the clock running on double airline schedules. "Every day it rose another inch higher. Until it got so high it sealed her in entirely. Cut her off entirely. Left me on the outside. And I wasn't able to reach through to help her. And I hated her for making me feel so helpless. I hated her for having something that shut me out. I hated her for allowing something to come between us. And then I never got a chance to tell her how sorry I was for hating her." I finished with my mouth dry.

She tilted her head, explaining it away by letting it slide off her shoulder with, "That's common with a lot of terminal patients."

I changed my mind about revealing how I had discovered afterwards that Judith had hidden medication rather than take it.

The glow was tapering out of the sunset, as if water had been dumped into it to extinguish it.

I took some comfort from the diminished light on my face, feeling somehow less exposed, less humiliated by my confession. Less vulnerable. I did not want to plead for her sympathy. Or plead at all. Pathetic. I shuffled to tie the faulty fragments of my confession back into myself, seeking to make them run through to us in this place.

"All it left me with was anger. And then loneliness. Like sometimes I wouldn't be able to take my next breath unless I could get her back." It came out untidy. Inadequate. "I'm sorry I'm like this. I am. Being with you. What you've made me feel. Is that I don't want my life to keep being like that."

"That might be a good reason for you. But not enough for both of us."

I pushed on despite her denial, nothing left to lose. "I can't believe you came away from last night with nothing."

"That's my business."

"You came away with nothing?"

"I might have."

"You realize what you're telling me to think about you? If you ask me to believe that?"

Her eyes jerked against the ebbing light, the whites like sliced moons. "Fuck you."

"Did you?"

She froze. Struggled, her jaw clamped shut. My quick words had wounded her.

She lost a tear from each eye.

From how they flustered her, I realized that she never let anyone witness them.

Without thinking I touched the wetness on her cheeks with my fingertips. "I'm sorry."

"Is this it?" she mumbled. "What you want?"

"No," I admitted.

"This is how it will be every time you have to wait for me when I cancel every evening we try for because I don't come home until midnight. Or come home too exhausted to talk. Or come home too upset to meet any of your needs. Or do anything else. Or don't come home at all."

"Maybe you'll end up waiting for me."

"That's not the same?"

"Could we start with something simple?" I asked.

"Like?"

"Just try to stay in each other's lives for a while."

"Is that what you really want?"

"I think I'd like to try."

"Then," she said dryly, "you're going to have to do a lot better than last night."

I was confused by the sudden change in direction, by her fresh boundaries. "Sorry. I was nervous. I should have tried to focus on your pleasure a little more."

"Oh Christ, I'm not talking about that."

Her retort caused me to stumble. "Somehow I didn't think you were."

"I've had a bellyful of wounded men who retreat into themselves and never want to share anything."

The sharpness of her verdict spurred me. "How do you know I don't share?"

"Because you haven't told me the most important thing about yourself."

"Which is?"

"You're still in love with your wife."

I was shamed by her accuracy. "I'm sorry."

"So am I." She made a vague half-finished gesture with her hands, lost track of something that had caught her eye behind me in the darkening sunset. "Every half-decent man I meet. You all seem to be so emotionally crippled these days. What the fuck happened to you all?"

"Life."

"I worry about what my sons are going to become."

I had no response for that.

"I want to change," I told her.

"Why?"

It would not come to me in words. How did I tell my life in less than a lifetime?

She stopped. Waited. In the waiting, our alternating breaths settled like falling feathers that collected at our impatient feet. Fear and frustration rippled in her face.

She declared, "I can't fill some gap left by your dead wife."

"What if," I attempted, "I could love you for who you are."

"It could be you really wanting someone to meet all your needs without you having to offer anything in return."

There was a beat. Our lagging hearts?

"And," she continued, "do you think you do after only one night? Love me?"

"I don't know. For sure."

"So what do you know for sure?"

"I know I need to be in someone else's life."

"Mine?"

"Yes."

"Why?"

"Because you're the one who makes me feel how I'm living now is not enough any more."

I watched her flick her fingernail at damp crumbs of mascara, no longer sure what else to do.

I shrugged. Sorry. Hated the sound of it inside my head.

She conceded with a sigh and a slackening of her shoulders.

I wanted us to kiss.

She came only as far as leaning her face into my shoulder.

I stayed with her. Close. Afraid to disturb anything for fear of stirring up our regrets.

Far from home.

25

I sat alone in the empty offices, the last to leave. Steeping in my complications and uncertainties. Trapped by my past promises. Suspended in time. Waiting for the clock to move so I could make my telephone calls to Bangkok.

Absently, I tapped codes, always firm in my memory, onto my computer keyboard. Before me, on my screen, Bloomberg charts flipped in a shiftless sequence of reports and graphs from the day's global markets. The strings of candy-coloured numbers throbbing loudly in pink and green and yellow. The market indices from Mexico City and Rio de Janeiro falling; New York and London rising; the numbers like some mistakenly inverted weather report where all the high-temperature digits were stuck to the cold locations while the cold-temperature digits were pasted to the southern climates.

I lifted my briefcase, set it on my desk, flipped it open. Within lay the clean shiny pages of contracts I had brought home from Bangkok Commercial Bank. I ran my fingertips over the smooth paper, lifted a corner with my thumb, and let the pages flap back into place.

I settled back, letting the cadence of my fingers on the keyboard decelerate, go soundless; letting myself, physically and emotionally, go inert.

In my stillness, I was certain of what I would do. How I would do it.

It was not a new idea. All of my ideas now lived within a single idea. Nor was it a new decision, or a new action. I had already defined my future actions within my past actions. With the money, when you had been holding an investment for too long, your only remaining action was to sell.

I was determined I would succeed. But in a way that I did not victimize others to protect myself from being victimized. In a way that I could remind myself about why I had come to work with the money in the first place, to tame it, build with it.

I closed my eyes to see it.

Was this the moment to do it?

And it was not like bringing anything closer or making anything clearer. It seemed more an uprooting of one decision from a place where two decisions were crowded side by side, so that the other could breathe freely.

I tried to talk through the logic and the rationales in the voice I spoke within myself, but that voice would not cooperate. I knew before I tried that it would only speak to my head, and not my heart.

Instead, it delivered up a lush memory of a fragile seashell lost from my fingers while I snorkelled in sunny waters, suspended above a reef off Nassau, the pearly half-moon fluttering down into the darker green depths until it vanished in the shadow of some coral. My sadness and sense of loss, as I watched the shell disappear, suddenly overwhelmed by the comfort of remembering that, on the beach reading her book, someone loved me. My last recollection of feeling truly whole within myself.

After embracing the solace of that interior refuge for as long as I could, I reached to my telephone, dialled, soaring out around the world to where it was morning, bright and hot.

"Stanley. How are you on that idea?"

"Which one?"

"The joint venture. You. Me."

"Tell me about it."

"As we suspected, my people are cutting my throat because they've got the whole thing set up in a cosy little backroom deal in the Bahamas."

"Can you blow the whistle on them?"

"Wouldn't make a bit of difference. It's not illegal for a deal to go south because the financing goes sour. Just bad luck. And there's no way anybody can trace them through the bank secrecy laws in the Bahamas. You know as well as I do that the Bahamas authorities might cooperate to flush them out if there was any suspicion of drug money. But they're rock solid. Swiss bankers behind them."

"So what do we do?"

"Can you get Benny Lim to change the financing? Swing it over to us?"

"Us?"

"Our new company? You and me. I can incorporate it tomorrow. With lawyers I know in Cayman. Where the funds are."

"For a price. Lose all of my fees. Maybe add another half million in the cost of funds."

"Then do it."

"That's being pretty generous with my fees. And our profits."

"We'll work it out."

"He'll only listen if we've got the Bangkok Commercial bonds and we've locked up the bond trust for a hundred per cent collateral. He's not about to take any risk on us."

"We'll get them."

"How?"

"I'll come back to Bangkok. Work it out with Bangkok Commercial. They need our cash."

"What's to prevent Amsterdam from offering the same cash?"

"They can't. Not unless they offer Bangkok Commercial more than we're offering. Which would mean Amsterdam would lose money on every bond order they fill. Because they've already pre-sold below market. Cut their own throat."

"You think Amsterdam's going to buy from us? Our little Cayman corporation?"

"Then let the fucking greedy bastards die out there. We'll sell the bonds ourselves. At market."

"That'll take weeks."

"What else have we got to do? We're launching our own company."

"That means keeping the funds out for a lot longer than two days."

"You'll have to negotiate that with Benny Lim. I know he'll scream. But you know his people are hungry as hell to get those funds out of Cayman and into a legitimate deal."

"And you know our exposure on those funds. We could be getting our hands a little dirty."

"When we're bigger we can get wiser. And have cleaner hands. Anyway, they're not exactly a cocaine cartel. It's more likely just investment profits that they've decided never to pay taxes on."

"Oh. Yeah. I'll be real happy going into the deal clinging to an explanation like that. I'll be sure to keep it in mind at all times."

"What other choice have we got? Fail? Let them win? Find some dead-end job outside the financial industry?"

(The logic was ragged around the edges. I had to force the pieces of the argument together. I tried not to let the forcing ferment in my voice.)

"Now you sound like my father and Uncle Benny."

"Sorry."

"They haven't exactly done too badly."

"It's just bridge financing for us. We take the money and sit on our asses, sell no bonds, nothing happens. We blow the bond deal. We fail."

"You've got that fucking right. Which scares the hell out of me."

"But we won't fail. And that's what I'm concentrating on rather than the source of the bridge financing. I can do this. I know I can. I can feel it coming back to me."

"The old juice. The old magic."

"Faster than a speeding bullet."

"You say so."

"And I'm tired of working for people stupider than I am."

"You got that part right."

"So we go."

"What about Bangkok Commercial?"

"I'll call Sanoh Sajjakul. Now. I'll promise him I'll be back within forty-eight hours. With the cash. You just promise Benny Lim that we're purchasing the bonds through our own company. That we can fully pledge them. Fully secure the entire deal."

"You really want me to promise him that we're purchasing the bonds when all we're really doing is warehousing and arbitrage?"

"Call it purchase. Call it anything you want. Just promise him we'll be there. With the bonds. With the deal. With everything."

"When?"

"Stay where you are in Hong Kong. Set a meeting for the end of this week. Friday afternoon. I'll be there. With everything."

"You don't show, call me the week after in Beijing. I'll be working at Bank of China."

"I'll be there."

"Can't say it's not going to be an interesting week."

I held the receiver for several seconds after Stanley hung up, seeking some reassurance in the constant hum of the dial tone. No reassurance came. I dropped the receiver into the cradle, slowly opening my fingers to empty my hand of the evidence.

Not betrayal.

Business.

Although I knew I had crossed some threshold, I could not sense if it was entry or exit. Although I knew that I was now changed by what I had done, I could not seem to feel it sufficiently. The emotion inordinate to the action. And that part, I recognized, was because the money never allowed them, all my feelings, to come to me when I was working it, the money, into the world—violent paint onto an unruly canvas. But the consequences would endure with me. I understood that part. They would stay with me. And, rather than reveal themselves all at once, they would accumulate in me during the rest of my life. In my actions now, I was burning my ships on the shore; there was no going back.

Returning to the second computer on my desk, the one not networked into the primary server, the one where I kept my deal files, I repositioned myself solidly square with the keyboard, cutting off any field of vision other than my screen. I spread my fingers, raised them over the keyboard. Took a weary breath. I let my fingers descend, working their drudgery against the heaps of yellow file icons and white commands popping up onto the black screen. Erasing all of my files and information. Reformatting the hard drive to obliterate any trace that I had ever existed. Like having my footprints within the firm swept away by an invisible hand.

Knowing I was leaving one life for another life.

Wanting to leave one self for another self.

Hoping to silence the voice in the process.

26

There was a limit to what I could do, how far I could go.

Luggage dropped inside the door. Without light, I went into the living room, stood in the window, feeling as if I was in danger of being sucked out through some imperfection in the glass into the cold Toronto night. Deeply dark outside. The stars shut out by a roof of tightly packed cloud. More snow imminent.

When I broke away, I was unable to estimate how long I had remained there, only that my calves and the small of my back ached from the standing.

I forced myself to leave the living room before I was snared by the television set, my night expended in bobbing like a cork in the currents of hour-long commercials for country music collections and fat-free cookware, submerging into troubled dreams only for as long as I could hold my breath. I began moving through the apartment, testing my return to its sealed atmosphere in stages.

Unsatisfied and needing, I roamed towards the bedroom, my steps first by default, then by design.

I entered cautiously, as if I were intruding into someone else's home.

I turned on the small bedside reading lamp, too exhausted to tolerate anything brighter.

I approached the dresser where most of her clothes remained. Slowly, I inched out the drawers I had previously been afraid to open, as if going over the lip of the drawer would take me off the edge of the world.

I let my palms sink into her cold, folded things.

I lifted twin balls of faded cotton tennis socks, weighing them in each hand, hoping somehow to measure my ability to live out the rest of my life with my dead wife.

Bitterness walloped me.

I let the socks flop back into the drawer.

But I had held in my hands things that she had held in her hands.

If I could begin with that much I could make up the rest as I went along.

I backed up, sat on the edge of the bed. I lifted the bedside telephone receiver. Extracted my wallet and dialled a number scribbled onto the back of a business card.

Her voice poured out to me in fruity tones.

"It's Wilma. I'm not here. Leave a message and I'll call you back. Bye for now."

I could not.

Yet I dialled a second time in order to draw the recorded tracings of her voice deeper into my head.

And, on her second invitation, managed to report in meticulously restrained eagerness, "Hi… it's me… Thought I'd let you know I got home okay… Just wanted to tell you that over on this side of the world… I'm still thinking about you… I've got to jump back on a plane in the morning and leave again… But I'll be back the same time you get home in another week… I'd like that...I'd like that very much...Both of us getting to the same place at the same time."

I settled the receiver gently, not wanting any harsh noise to go to her with my message.

Sluggishly, I pushed myself to my feet, went over to the closet. Retrieved my tangled duvet and crushed pillow. Headed for the living room. Stopped in the doorway. I turned to the bed. Studied it. I came back to the bed. Undressed. Pulled back the covers where they bore the dent of my seated telephone call. Got in. Snapped off the light.

I lay there, waiting in the darkness.

I was tired.

And I hurt more than I knew how to describe within myself.

I did not know how to locate what would come next.

I closed my eyes.

I felt the next minute pass.

And then I felt another follow.

Credits

A novel begins as thought and emotion; and writing is a solitary process; but publishing is a collaborative effort. To my publisher, Patrick Boyer, and his dedicated team at Blue Butterfly Books for their contributions, support, and commitment in bringing my novel to light of day, thank you.

F.W. VOM SCHEIDT's education, experience and career have embraced the author's broad spectrum of interests, from film and philosophy to mathematics and economics.

Before entering the investment industry, he held university and corporate appointments in marketing and finance, always with a core focus on fostering creativity and entrepreneurship. For more than a decade, vom Scheidt has been a director of an international investment firm.

The author works and travels in the world's capital markets, but makes his home in Toronto, Canada.

Interview with the Author

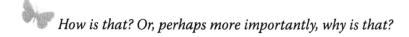 *With the global financial meltdown and everyone's quest for cash, this seems a highly topical book because we are all "coming for money." Yet although money has values printed on bills and stamped on coins, you seem to say something quite different. To you, what is the value of money in the life of a person?*

F.W. VOM SCHEIDT: The question might better be: What is the value of money in human life where we all face certain mortality? The ultimate futility of the acquisition of material things that do not accompany us in death is obvious. The misery of poverty is obvious. The merit of altruism is obvious. Despite all these truths, the value of the money itself remains, for most human beings, mired in layers of greed and fear.

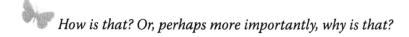 *How is that? Or, perhaps more importantly, why is that?*

VOM SCHEIDT: When you strip away the material acquisitions, recognition, and status that are the transient rewards of greed, and expose that we can be as easily hated as admired for the accumulation of money, you are still left with the paradox that we seek money to measure the progress of our endeavours, to improve the circumstances of our lives, and to protect ourselves and the people in our lives from future adversity.

 So what's left?

VOM SCHEIDT: Working every day in close proximity to money, I was forced to spend a great deal of time and thought on that very question, if for no other reason than to construct some sense of meaning in my own life. Over the years the answer that came to me was that the value of money to a person is that money accelerates experience.

 Accelerates experience?

VOM SCHEIDT: It's a concept that begins with recognizing that the most precious thing in this life is time, because our time is limited by our death. We cannot buy more time with our money. But, like Albert Einstein's theories for uniting space and time into space-time and "bending" the velocity of space-time, in a parallel way we can increase the amount of time in our lives by combining experience and time into experience-time. We can "stretch" the amount of our experience-time by accelerating the amount of experience in it. And that is the value of money.

 If that's the theory, how does it work?

VOM SCHEIDT: Imagine two men living in separate huts by a river. For both, the experience quotient in their lives is the sum of the experience of living in the hut and the experience of walking from the hut to the river and back fetching water each day. Through some fortunate circumstance, the second man acquires some money and buys a goat. The experience quotient of the second man begins to increase, because now he is bringing food and water to the goat, watching the goat grow, milking the goat, making cheese from the goat's milk, walking miles to a market to sell the cheese, taking in all of the sights along the way, and hearing other voices and other opinions in the market. The result is an exponential increase in the second man's experience quotient.

Meanwhile, the experience quotient of the first man remains the sum of the hut and river. Two lives with an equal amount of time measured by an equal number of days, but the second life has much denser experience. Because money accelerated the experience in the second man's life by increasing experience-time, even this simplistic example illustrates the value of money in enriching our life.

Moving from the personal experience of someone who is empowered by money to lead a richer range of experiences in life to the larger impersonal picture, however, the money markets themselves seem quite ruthless or unsentimental in how they allocate resources. Is this your view?

VOM SCHEIDT: The markets themselves are not ruthless and unsentimental. In theoretical economics, markets are efficient, attracting capital where it will obtain the greatest return with the least amount of risk. But markets are "made" by human beings. As human beings do in all endeavours in this life, they bring an untold wealth of knowledge, talent, integrity, and imagination to financial markets. But they also bring the human weaknesses of greed and fear.

It is usually when the equilibrium between all of these things is lost that greed and fear become the driving forces in the financial markets. Greed and fear are ruthless and unsentimental in how they allocate resources to any human endeavour. As we have seen time and again throughout history, not just in the recent developments alone, when greed and fear drive markets into unsustainable levels, all such markets inevitably collapse.

I guess that's why, even though money markets are often spoken of as autonomous entities operating almost like a force of nature, in Coming for Money *you paint a portrait, really an insider's view, with humans very much present in the scene. Are you saying the general public perception of the world of high finance is incomplete or simplistic?*

VOM SCHEIDT: Very much so, just as simplifying or stereotyping any human endeavour is always inaccurate.

Then should a person whose life becomes enslaved to money—making it, taking it, manipulating it—be pitied, like any other addict who's lost control over his or her own life? Is that a message in Coming for Money?

VOM SCHEIDT: It is not the central message, but it is certainly one of the messages.

Because our societies equate financial success with a successful life, we are often blind to the inner stories of countless people in all endeavours who, in their desperate search for inner happiness, endlessly repeat a formula for financial success even while remaining deeply unhappy due to unresolved emotional and psychological issues at their core.

With the approach you take to money, and the philosophy you've just been expressing, do you feel Coming for Money *is breaking new ground?*

VOM SCHEIDT: At my last count, there are not many literary writers originating from the financial world. I write from personal experience. I write from what I know best.

In this novel I've written as truthfully as possible about the world of international finance, not with the over-dramatization so common in film and television, but with an intimate telling through a first-person narrative of what it can be like to labour in the world of money spinning... of how the money's immense leverage for triumph or disaster doesn't so much corrupt people as corrupt the way they treat each other... of how the relentless demands of the money so often deprive a person of sufficient time and energy to live through the events of their emotional and interior life.

Love lost can create feelings of guilt, bitterness, even despondency. Here you portray a character, Paris Smith, who is trying to carry on despite such a hole in the very centre of his being. Do you think this is common?

VOM SCHEIDT: I think we all suffer the "slings and arrows of outrageous fortune" in this life. I do, sadly, see many people succumb to this. But I also see many carry on. In fact, I have come to think that what is best about us, what may be our highest calling as human beings, is surviving and continuing and always summoning enough courage to take the next step in the journey of our lives.

When referring to "courage," do you see that as a defining attribute of surviving?

VOM SCHEIDT: Yes, but let's be clear about the complexity here. As much as this is a story of conflicts between people, it is also a story of the conflicts of a man with himself. He has doubts about his abilities. He has guilt about how he has failed and hurt others. He has the heartbreak of losing at love when he needs more than anything to be loved. He is angry at being betrayed in his marriage and in his career. He fears failure. He is, in short, living with many of the emotional issues that confront all of us in our daily lives. So that is why I have tried to tell this story in a way that will let others in our increasingly isolated society know that they are not alone.

It would be easy to feel oneself a victim in such circumstances.

VOM SCHEIDT: We hear a lot about victims in our era. That is why I have also tried to say something in *Coming for Money* about the value of not surrendering to the seduction of victimizing others, as a defence against being victimized. In writing a narrative about not giving up, I attempt to capture something true and evocative about how all journeys toward the light begin in darkness. I hope to offer readers some assurance that, in undertaking such journeys, they can become restored to wholeness, because that is what I believe. That is what I have witnessed.

How did you conceive of this particular character and his story?

VOM SCHEIDT: I sat down at the keyboard. Although I have always been a literary writer, I had no idea how I would capture my experiences in international finance through literary fiction. Without thinking, the first sentence came to me. I typed it. Then I looked at that sentence for a long time.

Instinct told me that the sentence had risen from something that was deeply absorbing me, and that it was something I had to tell. I knew I had to find some way to tell it truthfully. From that point, I knew there was no way out … except to construct the novel.

Hollywood makes movies about the glamour of money, and other writers have treated the lives of those caught in worlds of high finance they cannot control. What, if anything, sets Coming for Money *apart from those works?*

VOM SCHEIDT: While *Coming for Money* is a story that advances from chapter to chapter along the corporate intrigue that beats at its heart, and continually mirrors the financial headlines of our daily newspapers, it is much more. It is an illustration of what happens to us as human beings when we lose emotional connectiveness, when we lose emotional logic. I think that is somewhat different from writing about the lives of individuals caught in high finance plots they cannot control.

 Is this why you portray individuals imprisoned, not behind steel bars, but rather in what might be called their emotional cells?

VOM SCHEIDT: I illustrate in detail the plight of one man, Paris Smith, whose story begins in a state of emotional imprisonment—because he is tragically, if admirably, flawed. He is not flawed in the classic Shakespearean sense of a noble man who is brought to ruin by his own avarice or rage. His weakness is not that he lusts after wealth or power or flesh. Rather, and far more important for us in these times, he is flawed in that he never learned the great lesson of his generation: don't become emotionally involved! Smith's weakness is that he needs, and has always needed, emotional involvement in order to sustain his life. It is for him—as, ultimately, it is for us all—as necessary as breathing.

Is that emotional connectiveness the core of the story?

VOM SCHEIDT: Essentially, yes. I think that, as Paris Smith refuses to relinquish his search for emotional connectiveness, he becomes a character we learn to appreciate and admire. I hope readers will appreciate him as much as I do for the sometimes stubborn, sometimes creative, battles he wages against other men in his corporation who are pitted against him. In doing so, Paris Smith becomes ever more conscious of how he could stem his personal pain and loneliness. He might do so by simply retreating emotionally and victimizing those around him. Or he might learn anew how to offer up his own emotional involvement. I'll leave it for readers to see how this plays out in the end, and what moral they may want to find about the human quest in contemporary times.

Let's turn from Smith to you. Earning an MBA *is a common apprenticeship for entrants into the world of commerce and finance, but you arrived by a very different route as an artist, musician, and writer. Did this give you special sensitivity to understanding the pressures of big money?*

VOM SCHEIDT: I suppose it brought an emphasis on creating something of value, and a discipline to practise and concentrate on doing it well, like artists must. Seeking to capture life truthfully in any medium requires a dedication to integrity. That artistic code becomes a natural advantage when transposed to a business environment.

I found that a practice of concentrating on integrity brought a bedrock of truth and governance to my business management. I also found that it applied greatly to investment decisions, which not only require foresight and judgement, but also integrity of conviction to avoid the sway of greed or panic, and maintain clarity amid the noise and confusion of information overload. From this flows the value you add to the amalgamation of money and opportunity.

What about artistic sensibility or sensitivity? Did that transpose well also?

VOM SCHEIDT: My sensitivity has, perhaps, been in simultaneously understanding the pressures of money and in understanding people. The great fallacy of the financial industry is that its workings are accomplished with money. They are not. They are accomplished with people—people who need to be understood and valued, people with whom you must communicate. Maintaining sensitivity to people in an insensitive environment helps bring them to a common focus: on value, on integrity, and on success.

About this Book

How much money is too much? And how fast is too fast in life?

Investment star Paris Smith steps onto the top rungs of the corporate ladder, only to discover he is caught between his need for fulfilment and his need for understanding, between his drive for power and his inability to cope with his growing emptiness where there was once love. When his wife disappears from the core of his life, Smith's loneliness and sense of disconnection threaten to overwhelm him. When he tries to compensate by losing himself in his work, he stumbles off the treadmill of his own success, and is entangled in the web of a fraudulent bond deal that threatens to derail his career and his life.

Forced to put his personal life on hold while he travels nonstop between Toronto, Singapore, and Bangkok to salvage his career, the embattled financier is deprived of the time and space he needs to mourn the absence of his wife and to objectively assess his future options.

In the heat, turmoil, and fast money of Southeast Asia—half a world from home and half a life from his last remembered smile—Paris Smith finds duplicity, comradeship, and power. He also finds a special woman who might heal his heart.

The gripping tale is told by a talented new author, F.W. vom Scheidt, who has confidently crafted a fast-paced, highly readable novel. His details are fascinating. His characters are real and not easily forgotten.

CPSIA information can be obtained
at www.ICGtesting.com
Printed in the USA
LVOW04s2339160516

488570LV00023B/213/P

9 780978 498283